Sophocles

Oedipus Tyrannos

THE NORTON LIBRARY

Oedipus Tyrannos

EMILY WILSON is Professor of Classical Studies and Graduate Chair of the Program in Comparative Literature and Literary Theory at the University of Pennsylvania. Wilson attended Oxford University (Balliol College, B.A., and Corpus Christi College, M.Phil.) and Yale University (Ph.D.). In 2006, she was named a Fellow of the American Academy in Rome in Renaissance and Early Modern scholarship, and in 2019 was named a MacArthur Fellow by the John D. and Catherine T. MacArthur Foundation. In addition to *The Odyssey*, she has published translations of Euripides, Sophocles, and Seneca. Among her other books are *Mocked with Death: Tragic Overliving from Sophocles to Milton*; *The Death of Socrates: Hero, Villain, Chatterbox, Saint*; and *The Greatest Empire: A Life of Seneca*. Wilson is an editor of *The Norton Anthology of World Literature* and an advisory editor of the Norton Library.

THE NORTON LIBRARY

2021–2022

Euripides, Medea
  Translated by Sheila Murnaghan

Sophocles, Oedipus Tyrannos
  Translated by Emily Wilson

Aristophanes, Lysistrata
  Translated by Aaron Poochigian

Murasaki, The Tale of Genji
  Translated and Abridged by Dennis Washburn

Locke, Second Treatise of Government
  Edited by A. John Simmons

Rousseau, Discourse on the Origin of Inequality
  Translated by Julia Conaway Bondanella and Edited by Frederick Neuhouser

Shelley, Frankenstein
  Edited by Michael Bérubé

Mill, Utilitarianism
  Edited by Katarzyna de Lazari-Radek and Peter Singer

Dostoevsky, Notes from Underground
  Translated by Michael R. Katz

Woolf, Mrs. Dalloway
  Edited by Merve Emre

For a complete list of titles in the Norton Library, visit
wwnorton.com/norton-library

THE NORTON LIBRARY

Sophocles
Oedipus Tyrannos

Translated by
Emily Wilson

W. W. NORTON & COMPANY
Independent Publishers Since 1923

W. W. Norton & Company has been independent since its founding in 1923, when William Warder Norton and Mary D. Herter Norton first published lectures delivered at the People's Institute, the adult education division of New York City's Cooper Union. The firm soon expanded its program beyond the Institute, publishing books by celebrated academics from America and abroad. By midcentury, the two major pillars of Norton's publishing program—trade books and college texts—were firmly established. In the 1950s, the Norton family transferred control of the company to its employees, and today—with a staff of five hundred and hundreds of trade, college, and professional titles published each year—W. W. Norton & Company stands as the largest and oldest publishing house owned wholly by its employees.

Copyright © 2022 by W. W. Norton & Company, Inc.

Editor: Pete Simon
Associate Editor: Katie Pak
Editorial Assistant: Olivia Atmore
Project Editor: Maura Gaughan
Compositor: Westchester Publishing Services
Manufacturing by LSC Communications
Book design by Marisa Nakasone
Production manager: Jeremy Burton

Library of Congress Cataloging-in-Publication Data

Names: Sophocles, author. | Wilson, Emily R., 1971–, translator.
Title: Oedipus Tyrannos / Sophocles; translated by Emily Wilson.
Other titles: Oedipus Rex. English (Wilson) | Norton library.
Description: New York, N.Y. : W. W. Norton & Company, 2022. | Series: The
    Norton Library | Includes bibliographical references.
Identifiers: LCCN 2021037427 | **ISBN 9780393870855 (paperback)** |
    ISBN 9780393885316 (epub)
Subjects: LCSH: Oedipus (Greek mythological figure)—Drama. | Royal
    houses—Greece—Thebes—Drama. | Thebes (Greece)—Kings and
    rulers—Drama. | LCGFT: Drama. | Tragedies (Drama)
Classification: LCC PA4414.O7 W55 2022b | DDC 892.7/2609351—dc23
LC record available at https://lccn.loc.gov/2021037427

ISBN: 978-0-393-87085-5 (pbk.)

W. W. Norton & Company, Inc., 500 Fifth Avenue, New York, N.Y. 10110
www.wwnorton.com

W. W. Norton & Company Ltd., 15 Carlisle Street, London W1D 3BS

1 2 3 4 5 6 7 8 9 0

Contents

Introduction

The Plot

Many first-time readers of Sophocles' play will already know the shocking skeleton of Oedipus's story: he killed his father and married his mother, and had children with her, without knowing what he was doing. The mythical background is familiar to readers today, and would have been well known in its broad outlines to Sophocles' original audience. This is a drama not of surprise, but of suspense: we watch Oedipus discover the crucial buried truth about himself and his parentage, of which he, unlike us, is ignorant. The mystery that is gradually revealed to the spectators in the course of Sophocles' play is not what the leader of Thebes has done, but how he will discover it and how he will respond to this terrible new knowledge.

The legend goes that Laius, son of Labdacus and ruler of Thebes, learned long ago from the Delphic oracle, sacred to Apollo, that his son would kill him. When Laius had a son by his wife, Jocasta, he gave the baby to a shepherd to be exposed on Mount Cithaeron. Exposure, a fairly common practice in the ancient Greek world, involved leaving a baby out in some wild place in the knowledge that it would likely die. The practice allowed parents to dispose of unwanted children without incurring the blood guilt of killing a family member directly. Laius increased the odds against the child's survival by piercing and binding his feet so there was no chance he could crawl away. This detail of the myth seems to imply that the child was already several months old, although exposure was supposed to be performed on neonates. Like many elements of the Oedipus story, it is not very plausible: it is likely a detail added to the story to explain his name, which was imagined to come from the verb *oideo*, "to swell," and *pous*, "foot": Oedipus is the child with swollen feet. Exposure in real life almost always results in a dead baby; by contrast, exposed babies in ancient Greek myth and literature always survive, usually rescued by the kindness of lower-class or enslaved strangers. The mythical shepherd felt sorry for the boy and saved his life. He was adopted by the childless king and queen of Corinth, Polybus and Merope, and grew up believing himself to be their son.

One day, according to Sophocles' version of the myth, a drunken dinner party guest claimed that Oedipus was not the son of Polybus. Oedipus went to Delphi to seek the truth of the story, and the oracle warned him that he would kill his father and marry his mother. Oedipus fled Corinth and ran away, in the direction of Thebes. At a place where three paths crossed, he encountered his real father, Laius, without knowing who he was; they quarreled, and Oedipus killed Laius. When he reached Thebes, he found the city oppressed by a dreadful female monster, a Sphinx—part human, part lion, often also depicted in Greek art with the wings of an eagle and the tail of a snake. The Sphinx refused to let anybody into the city unless they could answer her riddle: "What walks on four legs in the morning, two legs at midday, and three legs in the evening?" She strangled and devoured all travelers who failed to solve the riddle. But Oedipus gave the right answer: "A human." Human beings crawl on all fours in infancy, walk on two feet in adulthood, and use a cane in old age. Oedipus revealed that he fit his name in a second sense: the verb *oida* means "I know" or "I have seen," so Oedipus the "Swell-Foot" became Oedipus the "Know-Foot." The Sphinx was defeated, and Oedipus was welcomed into the city as a savior. He married the newly widowed queen, Jocasta, and took over the throne.

When Sophocles' play begins, Oedipus has been ruling Thebes successfully for many years and has four children by Jocasta, two sons and two daughters. But a new trouble is afflicting the city. Plague has come to Thebes, and the dying inhabitants are searching for the reason why the gods are angry with the city. Oedipus, who dominates the stage from beginning to end, assures the desperate Priest and his young companions that he is entirely in control of the situation. He is the single ruler of the city, the man on whom all inhabitants depend, second only to the gods. He has already taken action and thinks he knows exactly what to do. The play traces the gradual process of investigation by which the buried family secret becomes public knowledge, and it shows how Oedipus's civic, social, and domestic power is undone, as is his confidence in his own superior cognitive abilities, even as he continues to struggle for control.

The play is often described as being about human agency and human knowledge. Oedipus has solved the riddle of the Sphinx, which is the life story of every physically abled human being. The play explores the possibility that Oedipus's ostensibly exceptional story might be a kind of parable for all human experience. After the protagonist has learned the truth, the Chorus treats his horrible journey from ignorance to knowledge as a paradigmatic instance of the precarity that characterizes all human lives: "O generations of mortals, / I count you as equal to nothing, / even when you are alive" (lines 1186–88).

But even in this same ode, the Chorus also insists on Oedipus's exceptional achievement (in solving the riddle of the Sphinx) and his exceptional power, telling him, "you have received the greatest of honors" (line 1203). Oedipus may be in certain ways paradigmatic of all humanity, but he is not at all typical. Sophocles is interested in the intersection between Oedipus's vulnerability, which we all share, and his extraordinary privilege—as well as his extraordinary curse. Oedipus can be seen as an extreme test case of the idea that all "generations of mortals" are blindly subject to the vicissitudes of fortune and the unknown will of the gods. On the other hand—and the play allows for both of these incompatible possibilities—the story of Oedipus can represent the specific pitfalls that adhere to a position of extraordinary privilege. Enslaved people, women (including those who are not enslaved), and less powerful men are represented as quite different from Oedipus, because they never imagined they could do and know everything.

Historical Contexts and Politics

We do not have any external evidence for the exact date of *Oedipus Tyrannos*. It is usually dated to around 429 B.C.E., because the plague with which the play begins is not a traditional part of the Oedipus myth, but seems highly reminiscent of Thucydides' description of the great plague at Athens, which struck in 430 B.C.E.[1] The opening descriptions of the horrific suffering caused by disease would have been personally shocking to audience members in a city that had recently lost about a quarter of the population to the same kind of devastating plague. If this dating is right, the representation of plague in Thebes, right after the plague in Athens, would have underlined one of the central questions the play poses to its Athenian audience: whether Thebes is like or unlike Athens.

In terms of political structure, the real Athens and the mythical Thebes initially seem quite different. Athens was a direct democracy: all adult male citizens had the right to speak in assembly meetings, to vote directly in important decisions (such as whether to go to war), and to be elected to public office (by vote or by lot, depending on the office). Athenian male citizens had far more microscopic personal control over the actions of their political community than the citizens of modern representative democracies. By contrast, the Thebes of the play is presented as a society in which a single individual (*tyrannos*) is the ruler. But there seems to be some meaningful confusion about whether all the Thebans are equally willing to acknowledge Oedipus's absolute authority.

Oedipus defines himself as a one-man ruler, a *tyrannos*, as do those around him. The word did not have the same connotations in

---

1. Some scholars have disputed this dating; for instance, Bernard Knox argues in "The Date of the *Oedipus Tyrannus* of Sophocles" (*American Journal of Philology* 77.2 [1956]: 133–47) that the play may have been composed in 425, after a later outbreak of disease in the city. Others have argued, unconvincingly, that this kind of reference to contemporary events is antithetical to tragedy and that therefore the play must have been performed in a year when plague was not on the minds of citizens. See also Robin Mitchell-Boyask, *Plague and the Athenian Imagination* (Cambridge, Eng.: Cambridge UP, 2008).

fifth-century Greek as its English derivative "tyrant," which always suggests illegitimate and abusive exertion of power (as do near-synonyms like "dictator" or "autocrat"). The word *tyrannis* ("one-person nonhereditary government") is not necessarily negative, although from the perspective of Athenian democrats, it often could be; Sophocles' audience would have included men who sympathized with nondemocratic systems of government, such as oligarchy and tyranny. The word *tyrannis* implied a system in which one person ruled without sharing power, as opposed to an oligarchy ("rule of the few," in which a limited number of people, usually wealthier and more privileged people, share power), or democracy ("rule of the people," in which many people, including some who are less wealthy, share power; "many" did not, of course, mean everybody; the majority of inhabitants in Athens—including all enslaved people, women, and immigrants—were exluded from democratic participation). The word "equal"—*isos*—recurs multiple times in Sophocles' tragedy, reflecting a concern over whether anyone else is equal to Oedipus. Oedipus insists on his own singularity. But Tiresias, the blind old prophet who knows the signs of the gods, declares, "Even if you are sovereign [*tyrannos*], still the right / to answer must be equal [*isos*]" (lines 407–8)—a principle that echoes the Athenian right, afforded to all citizens in the democracy, of *isogoria*, or "equal right to speech in public." Creon, Oedipus's brother-in-law, seems suspicious of Oedipus's desire to assert lone, superior authority over his equals; he implies that Thebes is less democratic than oligarchic, in that power might be shared between the three members of the royal household (Oedipus, Jocasta, and Creon). The play creates an important ambiguity about what exactly the political system of Thebes is or ought to be.

Moreover, a fourth system of government was also common in the ancient world: hereditary monarchy, or *basileia*. In political terms, the central irony of the play is that Oedipus imagines that he is a *tyrannos*—a ruler with no dynastic claim to the throne of Thebes—and discovers only far too late that he is actually a *basileus*, a king whose father was the previous ruler. The play's common Latin title, *Oedipus Rex*, and its anglicization, *Oedipus the King*, are therefore spoilers.

Sophocles' Oedipus has often been compared to one of Athens's own most famous and dominant leaders: Pericles, who served as a leader and general (*strategos*) in the city-state from the 460s to his death by plague in 429 B.C.E. Pericles was a dominant figure in the city for several decades; he expanded democratic institutions and pushed for strategies of military expansion. In 451, Pericles advocated for new citizenship laws, which mandated that Athenian citizens must have two citizen parents. This meant that Pericles' own children by his partner Aspasia, who was an immigrant with permanent resident status (the Athenians called them "metics"), became ineligible for citizenship. Oedipus imagines that his children are, like those of Aspasia and Pericles, only half native-born; but he turns out to be wrong. The play explores a case where being too native, with parents who are too intimately connected to their place and to each other, is much worse than being half-foreign. The play is not making a direct comment or suggestion about public policy on immigration or miscegenation between native Athenian and immigrant populations, but it provides a mythical and dramatic language for thinking about these topics. Sophocles' Oedipus, like Pericles, is a decisive, charismatic man, whose public, political decisions conflict with the reality of his household. The play's preoccupation with the blurred distinctions between native-born and immigrant Thebans, and with the various ways that a child might be legitimate or illegitimate, resonates with the sociopolitical concerns of Athens in this time.

Sophocles seems to invite comparisons between the real Athens and the mythical Thebes. Oedipus himself has qualities that many Athenian men in the audience might have recognized in themselves. He is quick-witted, decisive, optimistic, irascible, self-confident, proud, patriotic, brave or rash, both pious and skeptical in his attitudes toward religion, and a committed believer in the power of human reason. The play is engaged, at least in sideways, looking-glass fashion, with current Athenian preoccupations of the mid-fifth century. If the usual dating is correct, the play was produced at the very beginning of Athens's decades-long war with Sparta and its allies—the Peloponnesian War (431–404 B.C.E.)—fought for imperial dominance of the Greek-speaking world. As Thucydides evokes in his fictionalized version of a speech given by Pericles in the first year of the war, it was a time of enormous pride among citizens in

Athens's ability to fight off invaders, to expand its imperial dominance, and to maintain social and political systems that were imagined to be superior to all others in the Greek world. Sophocles could not have known how costly the war would be, in terms of the city's prosperity and the massive loss of human life; but his play hints at dark possibilities. A contemporary Athenian could have seen Sophocles' Thebes as a vision of how a proud, prosperous community could fall apart, partly as a result of its own overconfidence and lack of true introspection. Thebes could be seen as a world either away or all too near at hand.

Key Themes and Imagery

In his *Poetics*, the philosopher Aristotle—writing in distant Macedon a century after *Oedipus Tyrannos* was first produced, and probably basing his opinions primarily on written scripts rather than dramatic performances—describes the play as the finest of all tragedies. It includes two plot patterns that he thought were essential to good drama: a reversal of fortune (*peripeteia*) and a recognition (*anagnorisis*). Aristotle famously cites Oedipus as an example of someone whose fall into misfortune is the result not of bad deeds or evil character, but of some "mistake." The Greek word used is *hamartia*, which connotes an inadvertent failure to hit a target, like a dart that misses the bull's-eye. Twentieth-century critics often applied the different and modern concept of a "tragic flaw" to Oedipus, suggesting that we are supposed to see the disastrous events of the drama as fundamentally the protagonist's own fault; but this interpretation is not justified either by Aristotle or by the play. An important consideration against it is that in his later play *Oedipus at Colonus*, Sophocles makes Oedipus give a compelling self-defense: "How is my nature evil— / if all I did was to return a blow?" There is a clear distinction in ancient Greek thought between moral culpability—which is attached to deliberate, conscious actions—and religious pollution, which may afflict even those who are morally innocent. Readers must decide for themselves how far they think Sophocles goes in presenting Oedipus as a flawed, sympathetic, or even admirable figure.

Another popular modern approach to the play has been to see it as a classic "tragedy of fate," in which a man is brought low by destiny or the gods. Here, we need to be particularly careful to distinguish the myth—which can plausibly be seen as a story about the inevitable unfolding of divine will—from Sophocles' treatment of the myth in his play, which creates a more complex relationship between destiny and human action. Before Sophocles, Aeschylus had produced a trilogy that dealt with the family of Laius and Oedipus. This does not survive, but it likely showed the gradual fulfillment of an inherited curse. In Sophocles' play, our attention is focused less on the original events and their causes (the killing of Laius and the marriage to Jocasta) than on the process by which Oedipus uncovers what he has done.

Oedipus is defined from the beginning of the play as a clever man (*sophos*), the only person capable of solving the riddle of the Sphinx. Cleverness or wisdom—*sophia*—was a fraught topic in the culture of Athens in the 430s. "Sophists" (*sophistai*, "wisdom-teachers") had been coming to Athens for the past few decades. These men were usually, like Oedipus, immigrants from different Greek-speaking cities: for instance, Protagoras came from Thrace, Gorgias from Sicily, and Prodicus from Ceos. The sophists charged wealthy fathers fees to teach their adolescent sons new skills in rhetoric and analytical thinking, including (depending on the teacher) training in the nascent fields of metaphysics, epistemology, linguistics, ethics, mathematics, astronomy, and physics. The presence of new, sophistic forms of learning in Athens was a source of pride and suspicion. Some citizens worried that these clever outsiders might be destroying traditional Athenian family values and traditional religious beliefs—anxieties that would come to a head a generation later, in 399 B.C.E., with the trial and execution of Socrates, who was often seen as a sophist. Oedipus has a certain amount in common with the sophists in general and Socrates in particular: he is an exceptionally intelligent man who claims, ironically, to know nothing ("Know-Nothing Oedipus"). The play examines the costs and limitations of Oedipus's particular brand of cleverness, compared to the very different kinds of *sophia* and knowledge that the prophet Tiresias and the oracle at Delphi possess.

The riddle of the Sphinx defines humanity by the number of feet we use at different points in our lives. Sophocles seems to suggest that the name "Oedipus" is particularly closely associated with feet: as we have seen, it can be read either as "Know-Foot" (an appropriate name for the man who guessed the Sphinx's riddle) or as "Swell-Foot" (a reminder of the baby Oedipus's wounded feet). On the first interpretation of his name, Oedipus seems like an Everyman figure, a representative of all humanity: he is the one who truly understands the human condition. On the second, we are reminded of the ways in which Oedipus is not like us: his feet mark the fact that he was cast out by his parents, rejected from his city, and has, unwittingly, done things that seem to make it impossible for him to be part of any human community.

Like all Athenian tragedies, *Oedipus Tyrannos* was composed to be performed in the Theater of Dionysos, at the Great Dionysia, the civic festival for Dionysos, god of theater and wine. But the god who lurks behind the whole action of this play is not Dionysos but his brother Apollo, the god associated most closely with plague, prophecy, and the light of the sun, with enigmas and revelations. Gods sometimes appeared on stage in Athenian tragedy, but in this play, Apollo works always behind the scenes, and the human actors struggle to identify and interpret his mysterious will. Sophocles multiplies the number of oracles and messengers in the story, and Apollo presides over the complex unfolding of the truth.

Oracles are only one of many types of riddling, ambiguous, or ambivalent language used in the play, which is particularly concerned with all kinds of interpretation. Dramatic irony—a term that refers to moments when the audience hears a meaning of which the speaker is unaware—is another particularly important reminder that words may have more than one sense. For instance, Oedipus comments that Laius was "so unlucky / in fathering" (lines 259–60) and asserts, "I fight for him as if he were my father" (line 262)—speaking more truly than he knows.

The interplay between literal and metaphorical meanings forms an essential technique in the play. Sophocles creates a relationship between literal and metaphorical blindness, between the light of the sun and the light of insight, between Oedipus as "father" of his people and as real father to his own siblings, and between sickness as a physical affliction and as a metaphor for pollution.

Through linked patterns of imagery, Sophocles explores the central questions of who Oedipus is, what a family is, and what it means to be in a place or a community. Plague, disease, and blood exist; they are also recurrent metaphors for the state of corruption and pollution. The instability of circumstances is explored through repeated references to weather, storms, and the city as a ship, tossed at sea. Thebes is located inland, in central Greece; the image of the city at sea, tossed by the waves, conflates this mythical landlocked community with the real island city of Athens.

There are repeated puns and plays on the word "foot," especially in the opening scenes of the play, and on physical posture: sitting, standing, falling. It is as if Sophocles repeatedly challenges his audience to solve and resolve the riddle of the Sphinx, by reduplicating and reiterating the enigmatic fact that people find themselves in different positions at different moments: our feet hold us upright only temporarily. Hands are also important in this play, as the body part associated most closely with action and agency, especially with killing. The play makes us ask ostensibly childish but profound questions: whether we can depend on our feet and whether we are what we do with our hands.

The most important body part of all in this play is the eye, which is repeatedly associated with knowledge. The verb *oida*, "I know," is also the perfect tense of the verb "to see" (*idein*): Sophocles' play is a meditation on the close association in Greek culture, language, and imagination between sight and knowledge. The eyes are imagined to be the most reliable sources of clear knowledge; many Athenians would have assumed that autopsy, or eyewitnessing, ought to be the best, most reliable basis for information. But the murder of Laius, for which there was a surviving eyewitness, remains hidden for a whole generation, as does the story of how Jocasta's baby was exposed. The truth about origins, about guilt, about pollution, and about divine will turns out to be difficult or impossible to determine through physical eyesight alone. Oedipus begins the drama with two functioning eyes, but as the blind prophet Tiresias tells him, he is metaphorically "blind" to the truth. It is only by questioning and listening, using his ears rather than his eyes, that Oedipus finds his circuitous path to the truth. In the final sequence, after he "sees" the truth about his own past and his parents, he puts out his own eyes—and wishes he could also stop up his ears, to shut up all the orifices that provide cognitive access to the world.

This play, like all Athenian tragedies, was performed entirely by male citizen actors wearing masks; in the final scene, Oedipus must have worn a mask marked or blindfolded to depict his gouged eyes. The self-blinding provides a belated physical representation of the fact that Oedipus was, up to this point, metaphorically blind. At the same time, it also seems to be a counter to his earlier blindness—as if it is only by becoming blind like Tiresias that he can see the truth. Oedipus himself seems to suggest that he has blinded himself to assert his own agency: "self-handed, / I did it," he declares (lines 1331–32). In contrast to the unconscious, unknowing actions of killing Laius and sleeping with Jocasta, Oedipus puts out his eyes in full knowledge of what he is doing. But paradoxically, the self-blinding is also represented as a deliberate choice to give up knowledge and further vision, a refusal to look at his parents in the underworld. The final scene of the play poses the question of whether Oedipus is more or less in control of his own body—his feet, his hands, his eyes, his ears—now that he knows his own history, the history of his body.

Another central, ostensibly childish but profound question that runs through the play is, What is a parent? Oedipus imagines himself to be the biological son of Merope and Polybus, of Corinth; but they turn out to be his adoptive, not biological, parents. The story of Oedipus's exposure on the mountaintop as a tiny child prompts an ongoing meditation in the play about the relationship between two different models of parenting. Is a parent the one who produces or generates the child (like a seed—an image that recurs in the drama)? Or is the real parent the one who raises or cares for the offspring? The Greek word *trephein*—"to raise," "to nurse," "to take care of"—is associated with parents, but also with the childcare done in elite families by enslaved women, the nurses (*trophai*) who breast-fed and took care of little children.

One of the horrors of Oedipus's story, apart from parricide and incest, is the realization that biological parents do not always provide care for their offspring. Moreover, the play imagines the community of a city or country as another kind of family, with citizens as children raised or cared for by a fatherlike ruler. Oedipus seems, at the start of the play, to be the adoptive father of the Theban people. His real heritage, as trueborn son of Thebes, makes it impossible for him to foster the city without destroying it.

The bodies of babies, as the ancient Greeks well knew, are formed out of the bodies of their parents. There were competing medical theories in the fifth century B.C.E. about the precise mechanisms by which this process of generation happened, and specifically about whether both parents provide material to form the fetus, or just the father. The play's imagery creates very distinct ways of imagining fatherhood versus motherhood. Fathering is, in the images of the play, like planting a seed or sowing or plowing a field, or entering the "harbor" of a woman's body; the mother is like the field from which children are harvested, or the harbor into which boats enter. Jocasta's body is presented not in terms of what it can do or experience or be aware of (in contrast to the body of Oedipus); rather, her body is a place, one that becomes horrific when it is entered, used, or possessed by father and son. Within the narrative of the drama, Oedipus and Jocasta experience the same revelation and undergo the same journey, from ignorance to knowledge; both respond with violence against themselves, when they understand the truth about their own polluted bodies. But we are given hardly any access to the interiority of Jocasta's thoughts and feelings about her terrible family history; her body remains inside the house, not out on stage, and the Messenger emphasizes that Oedipus draws all attention from her to himself: "he made it / impossible to watch her suffering" (lines 1252–53). In the final sequence of the play, the association between female bodies and places is turned around: the daughters of Jocasta and Oedipus, the products of a body in which too many men have placed themselves, are seen by their father as pitiably placeless or unplaceable.

If the mother is like a place, places are also like mothers in this play; place-names and city-names in Greek are female, and the land is imagined as the mother of those who are born in it. Oedipus's uncertainty about his place of origin is represented as an uncertainty about his true mother: he is the son of Corinth, of Thebes, and of the crossroads where the three paths meet. He is also the child of Fate (another feminine abstraction), and most emphatically, he is born from Mount Cithaeron, the mountain that nurtured and saved him from death. In each case, the subaltern human beings who actually nurtured the child—the biological mother in whose womb he grew, the foster mother, the enslaved men who adopted and saved the baby—are erased from the narrative, and instead he is represented as born like the first humans of myth, from Mother Earth. An important myth in Athenian lore and ideology was that of autochthony: the Athenians boasted that their ancestors had always lived in Attica, in contrast to other, more diasporic Greek populations. Sophocles' Oedipus is a test case of the most extreme possible form of autochthony, born directly from the ground in multiple places. The play poses questions about where exactly a person comes from: the bodies of parents, or the earth, or the community?

A third childish, profound question running through the play is, How many? How many people are in your family? How many people are you? As we have seen, the play repeatedly uses terms for "equal," *isos*, and interrogates whether Oedipus is or is not "equal" to other members of the ruling elite in Thebes. Sophocles also creates an important confusion about how many people killed Laius; the testimony of witnesses is inconsistent on this crucial factual point. This is partly a useful plot device, to make it a little bit more plausible that the murder of Laius languished unsolved for so many years. But Sophocles turns it into a deeper thematic thread. Oedipus declares, emphatically, "One man can be equal to a group" (line 845). And the play traces ways in which Oedipus, through inhabiting many apparently incompatible roles in the city and in his family, is indeed equal to a group, a plurality: he is father and son, son and killer, ruler and outcast, savior and curse.

Athenian tragedy was performed in the open air, in a theater that included a large round dancing area, the *orchestra*, for the choral choreography, and a wooden stage called a *skēnē* that included doors to go in or out of the house or palace. Actors could enter or exit from three possible directions: stage left, stage right, and through the central stage doors. Entrances from off the sides of the stage—like that of Creon in the first scene—take much longer, such that the audience can see the character approaching for some time before she or he reaches the stage. *Oedipus Tyrannos* makes use of the dramaturgical possibilities of this space in its staging of the ways that other places affect and shape the central visible space, which is the public arena of Thebes. We have entrances from Delphi, from Corinth, and most momentously, from Mount Cithaeron, all of which affect and change the play's action—as well as exits and entrances from the house, the location of the marriage bed that has held Jocasta along with both her husbands. The stage itself becomes a new kind of crossroads, where multiple places and communities are joined together.

A play whose secret you already know might seem unlikely to be interesting. But it is impossible to be bored by *Oedipus Tyrannos*. The plot races to its terrible conclusion with the twisting, breakneck pace of a thrilling murder novel, while the contradictory figure of Oedipus—the blind rationalist, the polluted king, the dutiful killer of his father, the son and husband of Jocasta, the hunter and the hunted, the stranger in his own home—is a commanding presence, who dominates the stage even when he can no longer see.

The Playwright

Sophocles was a generation younger than Aeschylus and had an unusually long, successful, productive, and apparently happy life. He was born at the start of the fifth century, around 496 B.C.E., in the village of Colonus, which was a short distance north of Athens. His family was probably fairly wealthy—his father may have owned a workshop producing armor, a particularly salable product at this time of warfare—and Sophocles seems to have been well educated. An essential element in Greek boys' education at this time was studying the Homeric poems, and Sophocles obviously learned this lesson well; in later times, he was called the "most Homeric" of the three surviving Athenian tragedians. He was said to be a good-looking, charming boy and a talented dancer. In 480 B.C.E., when he was about fifteen or sixteen, he was chosen to lead a group of naked boys who danced in the victory celebrations for Athens's defeat of the Persian navy at Salamis. The beginning of his public career thus coincided with his city's period of greatest glory and international prestige.

Athens became the major power in the Mediterranean world in the middle decades of the fifth century, a period known as the "golden" or "classical" age of Athens. The most important political figure in the newly dominant city-state was Pericles, a statesman who was also a personal friend of Sophocles', and who particularly encouraged the arts. Pericles seems to have instituted various legal measures to enable the theater to flourish in his time: for instance, rich citizens were obliged to provide funding for theater productions, and the less wealthy may have had their theater tickets subsidized.

The prosperity of Sophocles' city took a sharp turn for the worse around 431 B.C.E., when the poet was in his mid-sixties. The Peloponnesian War, between Athens and Sparta, began in that year and lasted until after Sophocles' death. Soon after the outbreak of war, Pericles died in a terrible plague that afflicted the whole city. In the last decades of the century, the city became increasingly impoverished and demoralized by war.

Sophocles worked in the Athenian theater all his life. He made some important technical changes in the theater, including the introduction of scene painting, and the increase of the chorus members from twelve to fifteen. His most important innovation was bringing in a third actor (a "tritagonist"); previous tragedians had used only two actors. This practice allowed for three-way dialogues, and a drama that concentrates on the complex interactions and relationships of individuals with one another. The chorus in Sophocles became far less central to the plot than it had been in Aeschylus; this is part of the reason why Sophocles' plays may seem more "modern" to twenty-first-century readers and audiences.

Sophocles has also seemed "modern" in his acute depiction of human psychology and human relationships. The gods are largely absent in most of Sophocles' extant plays, and human beings struggle to interpret their obscure intentions. Sophocles' people are intense, passionate, and often larger than life, but always fully human. They often adopt positions that seem extreme, but for which they have the best of motives. These tragedies ask us to consider when and how it is right to compromise, and to measure the slim divide between compromise and selling out. Clashes between stubborn heroism and the voice of moderation are found in all Sophocles' surviving plays.

Contemporaries gave Sophocles' talent its due. He won first prize at the Great Dionysia for the first time in 468 B.C.E., defeating his older rival, Aeschylus; he was still under thirty at the time. Sophocles would defeat Aeschylus several more times in the course of his career. His output was large: he composed over 120 plays. The seven that survive include the three Theban plays, dealing with Oedipus and his family: *Oedipus Tyrannos*, *Antigone*, and *Oedipus at Colonus*. These were written at intervals of many years, and were never intended to be performed together. The other four surviving tragedies are *Ajax*, about a strong-man hero who is driven mad by Athena—and the consequences of that madness; *Trachiniae*, about Heracles' agonizing death by mistake at the hands of his jealous wife, Deineira; *Electra*, which focuses on the unending grief and rage of Agamemnon's daughter after her father's murder; and *Philoctetes*, about the Greek embassy to persuade an embittered, wounded hero to return to battle in Troy. The dating of most of these plays is uncertain, although *Philoctetes* is certainly a late play, composed in 409 B.C.E. The judges at the Great Dionysia loved Sophocles' work: he won first prize over twenty times and never came lower than second.

Sophocles seems to have been equally popular as a person, known for his mellow, easygoing temperament, his religious piety, and his appreciation for the beauty of adolescent boys. We are told that he had "so much charm of character that he was loved everywhere, by everyone." He was friendly with the prominent intellectuals of his day, including the world's first historian, Herodotus. He participated actively in the political activity of the city; he served under Pericles as a treasurer in 443/442 B.C.E., and was elected as a general with him in 441/440 B.C.E. After the Sicilian disaster in 413 B.C.E., in which Athens lost enormous numbers of men and ships during a failed naval expedition in the Peloponnesian War, Sophocles—then in his eighties—was one of ten men elected to an emergency group formed for policy formation. Sophocles' participation in public life suggests that he was seen as a trustworthy and wise member of the community. He may have been responsible for welcoming Asclepius, the god of medicine, into the city's pantheon for the first time—which may perhaps be relevant for the central preoccupation with sickness, plague, religious pollution, and healing in *Oedipus Tyrannos*.

Sophocles was married and had five sons, one of whom, Iophon, became a tragedian. He was over ninety when he died. His last play, *Oedipus at Colonus*, is set in the place of his birth—Colonus, where according to legend, the polluted Oedipus came to find sanctuary in the holy grove of the Furies. This play about old age, acceptance, and redemption is a kind of sequel to *Oedipus Tyrannos*, but composed many years later. It was performed posthumously in 401 B.C.E., directed by Sophocles' grandson, also named Sophocles.

A Note on the Translation

Sophoclean tragedy is composed in a poetic style that is dignified, dense, and strange, but also smooth, fluent, and full of feeling. His metaphors are abundant, but not usually obscure. His characters seem like plausible inhabitants of a mythic heroic age, but at the same time are fully human. Their feelings are intense, and the plays often evoke terrible events and terrible suffering, but without bombast or a sense of melodrama. There is an aura of controlled, beautiful truth-telling in Sophocles' poetics. Virginia Woolf, in her great essay "On Not Knowing Greek," captures Sophocles' style in a marvelous image: "Sophocles gliding like a shoal of trout smoothly and quietly, apparently motionless, and then, with a flicker of fins, off and away."

I approached this project having completed translations of several very different texts, all, like Sophocles, in metrical verse: the tragedies of Seneca, four plays by Euripides, and *The Odyssey*. I knew I did not want to make Sophocles sound quite like any of them. Sophoclean tragedy is never as ornately rhetorical and allusive as Seneca. Sophocles was said to be further from ordinary speech than Euripides, and his plays certainly have less black humor. The language is intricate and literary, not based on an oral folk tradition like that which informs the Homeric poems—which are far more straightforward in their syntax and imagery than Sophocles. Within the limitations of my own literary and poetic capacities, I hoped to create for my English Sophocles a language that was fluent, humane, natural, and also markedly artful; sometimes conversational, but never slangy; full of puns, but not funny or unserious; always rhythmical, often rich in imagery, sometimes odd, but never stiff or unintentionally obscure.

Many modern and contemporary translators of metrical classical verse render it into prose, or stacked prose, lines laid out as verse but with no particular rhythm. As in my earlier verse translations, I wanted to use a regular meter for the dialogue passages, to echo the regular meter of the original, and to use a markedly different set of rhythms for the choral lyrics, so that the reader or listener can experience the shifts in linguistic music and emotional pitch without having to consult the notes. I kept as close as I could to the pacing of the original, but sometimes I found that my English needed to be a little longer than the Greek; the marked line numbers in this translation match the Greek rather than the English, to aid the reader who consults scholarly books or articles on the play. The original, like all Athenian drama, primarily uses iambic trimeter for the dialogue passages, a meter that was said to be the closest to normal speech; I used regular iambic pentameter, because it is the obvious literary equivalent, used within the anglophone tradition as the standard meter of dialogue in verse drama from the time of Shakespeare onwards. The original choral passages are in intricate lyric rhythms, which would have been set to music and accompanied by dancing. I did not attempt to create an exact replica of the lyric meters. Instead, I used mostly anapestic and dactylic rhythms, and a variety of line lengths, to ensure that these passages were legible and audible as very clearly distinct from the dialogue passages, and to tempt the reader, at times, to hear a melody, to clap or tap her feet to the beat.

In working on the opening scenes, it was the feet that caused me the most trouble. The feet, the hands, the eyes, the plows, the ships, the harvests, the hunting, but above all, again and again, the feet: the overwhelming abundance of imagery and punning, dark double entendres that Sophocles pulls off without inducing confusion, laughter, or groans. Modern English-speaking readers are likely to imagine that puns should have no place in serious verse drama, and indeed a prominent modern editor and commentator on the Greek play, R. Dawe, repeatedly insists that Sophocles' apparent puns are mere accidents of language, not intentional wordplay; Dawe seemed to hope to save Sophocles from any imputation of bad taste. But accidental punning on this scale defies plausibility. Sophocles really does repeatedly, insistently, set the audience to solve, yet again and again, the riddle of the Sphinx, by presenting, over and over, linguistic motifs of feet, standing and falling. I hoped to honor the metaphorical and linguistic richness of the original, without making it sound ridiculous, within the relatively pun-phobic cultures of the contemporary United States and United Kingdom. Sometimes I used wordplay that I hoped would hover, as the original sometimes does, between idiomatic and mysterious. For instance, when Oedipus asks what prevented the Thebans from conducting a prompt investigation into the murder of Laius, he uses language suggesting that there must have been some kind of problem blocking their feet (*kakon . . . empodon*). I had Oedipus ask about an "impediment," a word whose root comes from the Latin for "foot" (*pes*); my pun is perhaps a notch more subtle than that of Sophocles, catering to the more delicate sensibilities of a modern anglophone listener or reader, who may more readily be offended by perceived linguistic excess. Throughout the play, I wanted to honor Sophocles' interest in riddling, dense, metaphorical language. I hoped to make the verse fluent and comprehensible, but at the same time layered, often strange, rich in surprising images and turns of phrase. I felt the language should sometimes feel enigmatic, as the original does; enigmas are a central element in the linguistic form as well as the content of the play.

Beyond style, register, wordplay, and imagery, I thought hard about the characterization of each member of the cast, including the reasonable, desperate Priest; the cautious Chorus; the two contrasting slaves, the Herdsman and the First Messenger, one eager to tell his story and one terrified of its repercussions, both old men terrified of torture and death, after long lives defined by the will of their enslavers; Creon, the family man, eager to keep private business out of the public eye; Jocasta, the pious, attentive wife whose faith in gods and in marriage is destroyed; and the commanding, quick-thinking Oedipus, whose charm, intelligence, wit, and charisma should come across as clearly as his domineering self-absorption and paranoia.

One particular challenge in translating this play was the wealth of contradictory political vocabulary that runs through this most political of Athenian tragedies—all of which implies different political systems and different political assumptions than those that will come readily to the minds of contemporary anglophone readers. "Tyrant" is not a satisfactory rendering of the various instances of *tyrannos* and its cognates, because it is far more negative than the original terms. In the title, I left the word transliterated, to make the play readily identifiable. But I could not transliterate the political terms in the text; doing so would give the false impression that all Sophocles' nonpolitical terminology is easy to translate into modern English. I was tempted to use the words "president" and "presidency," which seem to me the most common, relatively neutral English words for a person with supreme political power. But these words, in the United States at least, usually connote a very different political system, in which the executive privilege of a single individual is checked and balanced by groups of elected representatives. I compromised with a range of words such as "sovereign" and "sovereignty," or sometimes "ruler," and "power" for the cognate abstract noun *tyrannis*. This dilemma is a single instance of a challenge that is constant for every work of literary translation. Languages are always entirely knitted up into their own social and cultural contexts, and translators grapple, in every line, with the vast imaginative gap between one culture and another.

The resonances of this or any classical text with modern culture will change as our culture changes. This play is about immigrants, about what it means to be an insider or an outsider in power, about the enormous privilege wielded by an elite man who still sees himself as an outsider or underdog, about the capacity of less privileged people in society (like the enslaved herdsmen) to change their government and bring down those in power, and about what it takes for their voices to be heard or to be silenced. It prompts us to ask whether we can or even should distinguish sharply between the public and the private self. It takes place at a time of a massive medical crisis, in which families are being torn apart and children are dying. It is about family structures, and about the cultural or natural boundaries between "normal" and "abnormal" presentations of gender and sexuality. It is about paranoia and the fear of conspiracies, and about an investigation that threatens to bring down the head of state. It stages confrontations between different kinds of expertise, different kinds of privilege, different modes of intelligence, different kinds of awareness, preparation, knowledge, and blindness. It prompts questions about the proper basis for power: qualifications, or the will of the people. It probes the relationship of political theater to political effectiveness and considers whether the appearance of quick, decisive, strong, solitary action, without consultation, is sometimes or always good practice for a leader. It interrogates the question that haunts all modern democratic societies, of whether those who hold public office need to be spiritually, personally, or morally pure in their private lives, and conversely, whether any private actions are bad enough to disqualify a person from public office.

Some elements of this ancient tragedy are very far distant from the concerns and beliefs of most people alive today. It is about the workings of a god, Apollo, in whom few of us now believe. The idea that inadvertently killing one family member and marrying another would inevitably cause terrible religious pollution is alien to most modern secular understandings of how the world works. Oedipus's road rage and involuntary manslaughter of Laius are unfortunate, and his relationship with his mother is the stuff of tabloids; but people in contemporary cultures would probably not see the ignorant perpetrator as "unclean," or imagine that his presence in our society would bring plague and divine rage. We are more likely to believe that the most horrifying human actions are those that are deeply wrong from an ethical rather than a religious perspective—such as genocide or slavery or torture or child abuse.

But on another level, Sophocles' play is entirely accessible to the feelings and imaginations of contemporary readers or audiences, as Freud, the psychologist who formulated the "Oedipus complex," well understood. We can all share the nightmarish terror that the confident pursuit of greater knowledge might lead to horrible discoveries of things better left unknown. Anyone who has lived past childhood or been guilty of terrible misunderstandings knows that a person's place within a family or community may change in unexpected, perhaps shocking ways. We are all aware of people, perhaps including ourselves, who have assumed that our privileges are based on our own merit, only to discover that we have made terrible mistakes. We can all understand the fear that there might be some hidden horror in our past, in our parentage or history, of which we ourselves are blithely unaware.

Sophocles: A Chronology

Sophocles produced over 120 plays, of which only seven survive. Hardly any of the dates of his plays are securely known. We have the titles and some fragmentary quotations from a number of the lost plays. Sophocles was never awarded lower than second place in the Great Dionysia competition, and he was given first prize eighteen times at the Dionysia, and six times at the Lenaea.

? 497/496 B.C.E.	Born, probably in Colonus, outside Athens, to a wealthy family; his father may have manufactured armor.
480	Battle of Salamis: Athens warded off attempted invasion by the Persian emperor Xerxes. Sophocles, then a teenager, was chosen to lead a ritual dance (a *paean*) in celebration.
470	Sophocles' first contribution to the dramatic competition at the Great Dionysia.
468	Sophocles' first victory in the dramatic competition; defeated Aeschylus.
443/442	Sophocles served as one of the financial managers (*Hellenotamiae*) of the city, under Pericles. Served in military campaign against the island of Samos.

441   Elected as one of the ten generals—leaders of the city—
           along with Pericles.
440s   *Antigone*; *Ajax*.
431   Outbreak of Peloponnesian War.
430   Major plague in Athens.
429 (?)   *Oedipus Tyrannos*.
420   Sophocles set up in his house an image and altar to
           Asclepius, god of healing and medicine—a new addi-
           tion to the Athenian pantheon. Received title of Dexios,
           "Receiver" or "Welcomer" (of the god).
415–413   Disastrous naval expedition from Athens to Sicily;
           vast casualties and enslavement of Athenian citizens.
413   Sophocles was elected as one of the members of the
           commission charged with determining the response
           of the city to the disaster, and deciding on appropriate
           repercussions for those in charge.
409   *Philoctetes*.
406/405   Death.
401   *Oedipus at Colonus*, written by Sophocles, produced
           by Sophocles' grandson.

Sophocles

Oedipus Tyrannos

Characters

Speaking Parts

PRIEST
OEDIPUS
CREON
TIRESIAS
JOCASTA
HERDSMAN
FIRST MESSENGER
SECOND MESSENGER
CHORUS *of fifteen male Theban elders*

Nonspeaking Parts

Children and acolytes (accompanying PRIEST)
Slave of TIRESIAS
Daughters of OEDIPUS
Bystanders

Oedipus Tyrannos

First produced ca. 429 B.C.E.

(*The* CHORUS *is present in the orchestra.° On the stage, the*
PRIEST *is gathered with acolytes and a group of young children*
beside the altar.° OEDIPUS *comes out of the palace—through the*
central doors behind the stage—to address the whole crowd.)

OEDIPUS
　　Children! Young ones nursed by this old city
　　of Cadmus!° Why are you all sitting here,
　　in wreaths and with those supplication branches?
　　The city is all full of incense, full
　　of groaning, and of songs, and prayers for healing.
　　I thought it wrong to hear this second-hand.
　　Children, I came myself. I am the man
　　well known to everyone, named Oedipus.
　　Priest, as an elder you should be the one　　　　10
　　to speak for all. What is your state of mind?
　　Are you afraid of something? Wanting something?
　　Indeed, I'd like to help with everything.
　　I would be cruel if I did not pity
　　the desperate way that you are sitting here.°

PRIEST
　　Lord of my country, Oedipus, you see us
　　gathered here at your altars—some so young
　　and weak, they cannot fly yet;° others heavy
　　with age. I am a priest of Zeus; these children
　　are special acolytes.° The other people
　　crowd in the marketplaces, wearing wreaths,
　　beside Athena's double shrine, and by　　　　20
　　the Ismenus, the oracle of ash.°
　　See for yourself! The city reels; its head
　　is sunk beneath the deep and bloody waves.°
　　The land is weakening: the seeds in pods

decay; the land is dying, and the cattle
die in the fields; the laboring of women
is birthless birth. The god who carries fire,
most cruel plague, is driving through the city
and emptying our houses, while black Hades°
grows rich on cries of grief and lamentation.   30
I've come here with these children to your hearth,
not thinking you the equal of the gods,
but as the first of men, in life events
and dealings with divinities. You came
to Thebes, the town of Cadmus, and released us
from paying the relentless Poet's tribute,°
though you knew nothing special, nothing extra;
we had not told you anything. Some god
helped you lift up our lives. This we believe.
Now Oedipus, most powerful of rulers,   40
we are all begging you to help us somehow.
Maybe you know some way to save us; maybe
you heard some god's voice, or some person told you.
I see that people with experience
manage to bring their plans to life most often.
So come, lift up our city! You're the best
of mortals. Come, be on your guard. The city
calls you its savior now, because you were
so helpful in the past. We would not want
your rule to be remembered as the time
we stood up straight, but then fell down again.°   50
Lift up this city and make sure it's stable.
Your bird of destiny brought us good luck;°
be the same now. You hold the power now;
if you would go on ruling, it is better
to govern in a populated city
than emptiness. A citadel or ship
is nothing, if no people live inside it.

OEDIPUS
Poor children! I already know all this:
why you have come, and what you want. I know

that all of you are sick with plague, diseased;°
but no one's sickness equals mine. You each   60
are only suffering for your own pain,
for your own self and no one else. My being
grieves for the city, me, and you, together.
You did not wake me. I was not asleep.
I have been crying late into the night.
My mind has traveled many different paths.
I looked intently, and I found there was
only one cure. I did it. I have sent
Creon, Menoeceus's son, the brother   70
of my own wife, to Delphi, to the home
of Phoebus,° to find out what I can do
or say to save the city. It is late;
the measurement of day against the time
makes me concerned how he is getting on.
He has been absent longer than he should.
When he arrives, shame on me if I fail
to do it all, just as the god reveals.

(CREON *appears from the countryside direction,° walking
toward the stage.*)

PRIEST
Your words are timely. Just this very minute
these children pointed Creon out to me.

OEDIPUS
Apollo! Lord! I hope his bright expression   80
implies that he is bringing us salvation.

PRIEST
It seems his news is promising; why else
would he be wreathed so lavishly with laurel?

OEDIPUS
We'll soon find out. He's now in hearing range.
(*Shouting*) My lord! My brother! Creon! What's the word
you bring us from your journey to the god?

CREON

Good news! I mean, if everything goes right,
all this disaster will turn out just fine.

OEDIPUS

Explain yourself. What you have said so far
makes me feel neither confident nor scared.　　　　90

CREON

If you want all these bystanders to hear,
I can speak now—or we can go inside.

OEDIPUS

Speak out to everyone. I feel more pain
for them than for myself and my own life.

CREON

Then I will tell you what I heard. The god
Apollo clearly says we must expel
pollution that is nurtured in this land,
not feed it till it turns incurable.°

OEDIPUS

What means of cleansing, what way out is there?

CREON

To impose exile, or pay death for death.
The land is feverish with this storm of blood.°　　　　100

OEDIPUS

Whose blood? What death? What does he mean by this?

CREON

My lord, before you came here, to this city,
the ruler of the country was named Laius.

OEDIPUS

I know, I heard about him; never saw him.

CREON

The god gives clear instructions: we must punish
the selfsame men whose hands killed our dead king.°

OEDIPUS

Are they in Theban territory? Where can evidence be
found of this old crime?

CREON

Here in this land, he says: the sought is caught,   110
and what is unexamined slips away.

OEDIPUS

Was Laius killed at home or in the country?
Was it in Thebes, or in some other land?

CREON

They say he went to seek an oracle,
and left, but never came back home again.

OEDIPUS

Was there no fellow traveler, no witness
or messenger with useful information?

CREON

All died but one; he ran away in fear,
and could say just one thing of what he saw.

OEDIPUS

What kind of thing? One clue can be revealing   120
if we can grasp the slender start of hope.

CREON

He said that with a multitude of hands
the robbers killed him. More than one attacker.

OEDIPUS

How could he be so bold—unless there was
conspiracy in Thebes, and he was bribed?°

CREON

It seemed that way. But after Laius died,
we had no one to help us in our troubles.

OEDIPUS

Power had fallen!° What impediment
prevented you from finding out the reason?

CREON

The enigmatic Sphinx made us abandon   130
puzzles, and look at what was at our feet.°

OEDIPUS

I will begin again and shed fresh light.
Apollo is quite right, and so were you,
to work so hard to help the murdered man,
and you will see me also fight for justice,
avenging both this country and the god.
I will myself for my own self dispel
pollution, not for distant relatives,
because whoever killed him might kill me   140
with that same swift avenging hand. So when
I help the dead, I benefit myself.
Now hurry, children, get up from those steps,
pick up your supplication wreaths, and someone
must gather all the Theban people. Tell them
that I will do it all, for if the god
is with us, we will have good luck—or fall.

PRIEST

Children, we can get up, because this man
has made the proclamation that we came for.
Apollo sent this oracle. May he
arrive to save us and to end the plague!   150

(CREON *exits.* PRIEST, *acolytes, and children rise and leave the stage by a side exit, as if for the city.* OEDIPUS *remains on stage, listening to the* CHORUS.°)

CHORUS°

What are you, sweet word of Zeus,
that traveled from golden Delphi to glorious Thebes?
I am quaking with fear; my heart is stretched tight with
   the terror.
Healer of Delos, Apollo our Healer,
you fill me with awe. What debt must I pay you?
A new one or something returned
from the circling seasons of time?
Tell me, immortal Oracle, child of golden Hope.

Daughter of Zeus, I call on you first,   160
deathless Athena,
and your sister, the earth-shaker, Artemis,
who sits on the glorious circular throne of the market,
and Phoebus Apollo, far-shooter;°
come and appear to me, triple protectors!
If ever before you banished the flames of disaster
from earlier curses besetting the city,
come now!

Horror! My sufferings
cannot be counted, since all of us,   170
all of the people are sick
and no sword of the mind can save us or help us.°
Our famous city
is increased by nothing. The women
emerge from their labors and shrieks with no children.
Like birds on the wing, one here and one there,
you see people sent faster than furious fire
to the shore of the western god.°

The city is dying, the dying are numberless.
There is no pity   180
for children who lie underfoot and bring death.°
The wives and the grey-haired grandmothers
jostle each other to clutch at the edge of the altar,
screaming their desperate

prayers of pain.
The chanting is shining and with it the wailing
of mourners is piping in harmony.°
For their sake, golden daughter of Zeus,
look with kind eyes and protect them.

Ares,° a fire, is burning me now in the din and the clamor   190
without shields or weapons of bronze.
Turn back his onslaught,
away from the bounds
of our fatherland, down to the spacious room
of the sea goddess, Amphitrite,°
or into the waves of Thrace,
which welcomes no anchors.
If night has left any ruin undone,
he does it when day comes.   200
Lord of the fiery lightning, Father Zeus,
blast him with thunder.

Wolf Lord, Apollo Lycaios,°
may the strings of your curved golden bow
scatter unstoppable arrows to help and defend us;
may Artemis blaze with the flames that she spreads
dashing through Lycian mountains.
And I call on the god
who is named after Thebes   210
in his circlet of gold,
the god with the wine-face, Bacchus,°
whose maenads whoop crowding around him,
to come with his dazzling pine-torch and burn
the god whom the gods are ashamed of.°

OEDIPUS

I know what you are asking. If you're willing
to listen to my words, and fix the plague,
you can get help, relief from all this pain.
I am a foreigner to this event,
and unfamiliar with what was said.°

The hunt would not have taken me so long   220
without a clue.° But now at last I am
a citizen, and I proclaim to you,
people of Cadmus: if you know who killed
Laius, the son of Labdacus, you must
reveal it all to me. And if the killer
is scared to blame himself,° his punishment
will not be too severe. He must leave Thebes,
unharmed, no worse than that. Or else if someone
knows that the killer came from somewhere else,°   230
he must speak up. I will make sure that man
receives his proper thanks and due reward.°
But if you do not speak—if anyone
pushes my words away, because he's scared
for someone close to him, or for himself—
listen to me! Whoever that man is,
I ban him from this land where I hold sway.
No one must let him in or speak to him
or share with him in sacrifice or prayer
to gods, nor let him touch the holy water.°   240
You must all push him from your homes. This man
pollutes us, as the Pythian oracle,°
the god, has recently revealed to me.
I fight beside the dead man and the god.
Whether the secret criminal did this
alone or with accomplices, I pray
that he wears out a poor, unlucky life
in misery.° And if that man has been
inside my house, and present at my hearth,
and if I know about it, I here vow   250
to take these curses I have made on me.
I lay it on you to fulfill all this,
for my sake, for the god, and for this land,
so ruined, barren, and unblessed by gods.
For even if the god had not compelled us,
it would not have been right for you to leave
pollution, from a well-born ruler's death.
It needs investigation. Now I have

the power that the dead man used to hold.
I also have his bed, and sow his wife
with him.° If he had not been so unlucky
in fathering, we would have common children.°   260
But Fate has leapt upon his head.° And therefore
I fight for him as if he were my father,
and I will do it all to seek and catch
the selfsame man whose own hands killed the son°
of Labdacus, the son of Polydorus,
the son of Cadmus, offspring of Agenor
in ancient times.° If anybody fails
to do this, I pray gods will send to them
no crops from earth, no children from their wives;   270
and let them die, from this plague, or from worse.
You other Thebans who agree to this,
may Justice fight with you! May all the gods
bless you and be with you forevermore.

CHORUS

Lord, I will speak, on pain of your own curse.
I did not kill him; I don't know who did.
Apollo sent the oracle; it was
for him to say who was the perpetrator.

OEDIPUS

Yes, what you say is right. But there's no man   280
able to force the gods against their will.

CHORUS

Let me say what seems second best to me.

OEDIPUS

Or even third best! Tell me everything.

CHORUS

I know that Lord Tiresias excels
at seeing as our Lord Apollo sees.

My lord, investigation in these things
would gain most clear enlightenment from him.°

OEDIPUS

I have already worked this field as well.°
As Creon told me to, I sent two men
to fetch him, and he should be here by now.

CHORUS

Good. All the rest is pointless, ancient rumors.   290

OEDIPUS

What rumors? I look into everything.

CHORUS

They say some people on the road killed him.

OEDIPUS

I heard that too. But no one saw who did it.

CHORUS

Well, anyone who can be touched by fear,
who hears these threats of yours, will soon be moved.

OEDIPUS

Words cannot scare one unafraid of deeds.

CHORUS

The man to prove his guilt is here; they're bringing
the prophet of the gods already—look!—
the only human in whom truth is planted.

(*Enter* TIRESIAS, *blind, escorted by enslaved helpers.*)

OEDIPUS

Tiresias, you see it all: what can   300
and can't be understood or spoken of
on earth and in the sky. Though you are blind,

you know about our city and the plague.
My lord, you are the only one we've found
to save us from it. If you have not heard,
we asked Apollo, and the god replied,
the only liberation from this plague
is if we find the murderers of Laius,
and kill them, or expel them from the land.
If you have information from the birds,°   310
or any other art of prophecy,
do not withhold it! Save yourself and me
and Thebes, and save the dead man from pollution.
We're in your hands. It is the best of labors,
to help another man as best one can.

TIRESIAS

It's terrible! How terrible to think,
when thinking does no good. I knew all that,
but I forgot. Or I would not have come.

OEDIPUS

What is it? How dispirited you seem!

TIRESIAS

Send me back home. If you do as I say,   320
we will both bear our lots more easily.

OEDIPUS

What? To deprive us of this holy word
is cruel and wrong to Thebes, your benefactor!

TIRESIAS

I see your words are heading for bad luck.
So may I not experience the same. . . .

OEDIPUS (*kneeling to beseech* TIRESIAS)
By the gods, don't deprive us of your knowledge!
We are your suppliants! We kneel before you!

TIRESIAS

Yes: none of you are thinking. I will never
reveal my ruin: I will not say "yours."°

OEDIPUS

What's that? You know, and will not speak? Do you   330
mean to betray us, and destroy the city?

TIRESIAS

I will not hurt myself or you. Why are you
asking these futile questions? I won't answer.

OEDIPUS

You evil monster! You'd enrage a rock!
So will you never speak? Will you keep up
this endless pose of rigid stubbornness?

TIRESIAS

You criticize my temperament, and blame me;
you do not know the one you're living with.°

OEDIPUS

Now you are disrespecting our own city!
Who wouldn't lose his temper at your words?   340

TIRESIAS

Even if I keep silent, it will happen.

OEDIPUS

So why not also tell me what will happen?

TIRESIAS

I would not say too much. Face up to that,
then rage your wildest, if you want to rage.

OEDIPUS

I am so seized by anger, I will not
shield you from what I think. Know this: I reckon

you helped to plant the crime, and even did it,
killing him, though not with your hands! If you
could see, I'd say the deed was yours alone.

TIRESIAS

Really? I tell you this: you must abide   350
by that announcement you yourself just made.
From this day on, you must not speak to us.
You are the cursed pollution of this country!

OEDIPUS

How dare you rustle up this accusation?
Do you think you can get away with it?

TIRESIAS

I have. The truth I raise is powerful.°

OEDIPUS

Who made you say this? Not your skill, for sure.

TIRESIAS

You did. You made me speak against my will.

OEDIPUS

What's that? Repeat it, so I'll understand.

TIRESIAS

Do you not understand? Is this a test?°   360

OEDIPUS

It doesn't make much sense. Say it again.

TIRESIAS

I say you are the murderer you seek.°

OEDIPUS

If you repeat that slander, you'll regret it!

TIRESIAS
Shall I say more, and make you angrier still?

OEDIPUS
Say all you want. Your words are meaningless.

TIRESIAS
You don't know how disgustingly you live
with closest family, and you don't see
how far you're ruined.

OEDIPUS
                              Do you really think
you'll get away with saying this?

TIRESIAS
                                        If there
is any strength in truth.

OEDIPUS
                              There's none in you!   370
Your mind and ears are blind, just like your eyes!

TIRESIAS
You poor, unhappy man. Soon all these people
will hurl these accusations back at you.

OEDIPUS
You are the child of endless night! You'll never
hurt me, or any man who sees the light.

TIRESIAS
It is your fate to fall, but not by me.
Apollo is enough. The task is his.

OEDIPUS
Who thought of all this? Creon? Or who else?

TIRESIAS

Creon is doing nothing wrong to you:
you are the one who's hurting your own self.

OEDIPUS

Sovereignty! Riches! Skill that can surpass   380
the skills of others, in a life defined
by competition! What a mass of envy
is hoarded up inside all these desires!
The city gave me, as a gift, the role
of leader—but I never asked for it!
But now for this position, loyal Creon,
my friend right from the first,° snuck up on me,
and wants to throw me out! He has coopted
this wizard, stitcher of conspiracies!
This lying beggar! Who can only see
where profit lies! He's blind to any art.
(*To* TIRESIAS) Come on then, tell me, how are you
   a real
prophet? When she was here, that song-composer,°   390
that dog, how was it that you did not speak
a word to free these citizens from her spell—
although the riddle surely needed skill,
prophetic art, not just some passerby?
Yet you did not show up with any knowledge
from birds or gods. Instead, I came along,
"Know-Nothing Oedipus," and I stopped her!
I hit the target with intelligence,
not getting information from the birds.
This is the man you're trying to throw out,
thinking that you will stand beside the throne
of Creon. But I think that you will suffer,   400
you and the man who put you up to it,
when you drive out this curse. If you did not
look like an old man, you would have discovered,
by suffering, the nature of your insights!

CHORUS

We reckon, Oedipus, that he was speaking
in anger; you were too. We don't need this.
Instead, look into how we may fulfill
Apollo's oracles, as best we can.

TIRESIAS

Even if you are sovereign, still the right
to answer must be equal. I have power
in speech at least, since I am not your slave;
I am Apollo's. Do not write me down   410
in Creon's list of immigrants.° I'll speak!
You have insulted me for being blind,
but you don't know the ruin you are in,
nor where you are or who you're living with.
Do you know who you come from? You don't see
that you're an enemy to your own people,
above the earth and under it. A curse
with feet of doom will strike you, from both parents,
and one day it will drive you from this land.
Now you see straight ahead; you will see darkness.
Your cries will resonate on every shore;   420
Cithaeron will be ringing with them soon,
when you know what your marriage is, and where
you smoothly sailed, to this perverted harbor.
You do not see the number of disasters
that will match you with you, and with your children.
You hurl this mud at Creon and at me,
but you will be washed out, annihilated,
crushed as no mortal person ever was.

OEDIPUS

This is intolerable! Must I keep listening
to him? You go to hell! Turn round, go back   430
out of my house, as fast as you can go!

TIRESIAS

I would not have come here if you'd not called me.

OEDIPUS

I didn't know you'd say such stupid things,
or I would not have brought you to my house.

TIRESIAS

I am like this: to you I may seem stupid,
but to your real birth-parents, I am wise.

OEDIPUS

What parents? Wait. Which mortal was my father?

TIRESIAS

This day will give you birth and bring you death.

OEDIPUS

Your words are all too riddling and obscure.

TIRESIAS

Aren't you the best at solving these enigmas?   440

OEDIPUS

You're mocking me for things that make me great!

TIRESIAS

No, but your skill itself will be your ruin.

OEDIPUS

But if I saved this city, I don't care!

TIRESIAS

I'm going now. (*To his enslaved boy*) Here, boy, take me away.

OEDIPUS

Away then! You are just a nuisance here.
Be off, and you will bother me no more!

TIRESIAS

I'll go, because I've said what I intended.

I do not fear your eyes. You can't destroy me.
This man you have been looking for so long,
Laius's murderer, that man is here.   450
He's called an immigrant, noncitizen,°
but he will be revealed a native Theban,
although he won't be glad about his fortune.°
Now he can see; he will go blind. Now rich,
he'll be a beggar leaning on a stick,
wandering through strange lands. He'll be revealed
the father and the brother of his children;
the son and husband of his own birth-mother;
the killer of his father, and the one
who shared his seed-place. Go in. Work it out.   460
If you find out it's false, call me no prophet.

(*Exit* TIRESIAS, *led by enslaved boy. Exit* OEDIPUS, *attended
by enslaved attendants.*)

CHORUS
Who did the things unspeakable, unspeakable,
with bloody hands of murder?°
Whom did the voice of the god,
the rock at Delphi, mean?
Now it is time for him to move his feet in flight,
faster than storm-swift horses.
The son of Zeus is after him, full-armed,
with fire and lightning bolts,   470
and with him come the Fates who never miss.

The word has now shone forth
from snowy Mount Parnassus
that everyone must track
the unseen man—the bull:° he wanders through
the wild wood, the caves,
and through the rocks, bereft, unhappy,
on unhappy feet,
fleeing the oracles from the earth's navel.°   480
But they live forever and fly all around him.

The wise interpreter of birds
has caused me terrible, terrible anxiety,
with words incredible and undeniable.
I don't know what to say. I fly on hope,
not seeing the present, not seeing the future.
I didn't know, I don't know now,
of any conflict that arose between
the sons of Labdacus and Polybus's son   490
to use as evidence, a touchstone test,
of Oedipus's public reputation,
to find out if I ought to help the Labdacids'
in solving their mystery deaths.°

But Zeus and Apollo are wise; they know and can see
the mortal world. There's no true judgment   500
to tell if a prophet is worth more than I am.
A man may surpass
wisdom by wisdom.°
But when people are blaming, I never agree
until I can see if their words are correct.
After all, she with the wings in the past
appeared to him, and by the test he was seen
as the wise one, sweet to the city. Because of this,   510
my heart will never discover him guilty of wrong.

(*Enter* CREON, *from the city.*)

CREON
I've come here, men of Thebes, because I learned
that Oedipus, our leader, has accused me
of dreadful things, and I won't stand for it.
If, in the present crisis, he imagines
that he has suffered any kind of harm
from me, in word or deed—then I do not   520
wish for long life, if I must bear this charge.
Indeed, this accusation brings for me
no simple punishment, but total ruin,
if I am called a criminal in Thebes,

and called a criminal by you as well,
and by my family and friends.

CHORUS

Come now,
the insult happened, yes, but it was maybe
forced out by anger, not by conscious thought.

CREON

But was it said in public that the prophet
was swayed by my advice to tell those lies?

CHORUS

Yes, that was said; but I don't know the motive.

CREON

And was he thinking straight and looking straight,
making this accusation against me?

CHORUS

I do not know, because I do not see   530
what those in power over me are doing.
But he himself is coming outside now.°

(*Enter* OEDIPUS, *from the palace.*)

OEDIPUS

You! How did you get here? Have you become
so brazen that you dare to show your face
and come to my own house, when you are clearly
the murderer of that man, and the proven,
flagrant thief who tried to steal my power?
Come on then, talk, by gods! Did you perceive
some foolishness or cowardice in me,
so you decided you would do this? Or
did you think that I wouldn't recognize
that it was you who made this treacherous plot,
sneaking against me—or when I found out,

you thought that I would fail in self-defense?
This plan of yours is stupid, isn't it?   540
To hunt for power, with no wealth or friends!
To get it, you need influence, and money.

CREON

Trade in your words for listening as an equal.
You need to understand before you judge.

OEDIPUS

I'm bad at listening to your clever words,
because I've found you mean and cruel toward me.

CREON

Just hear me out on this one thing, for once.

OEDIPUS

Just this one thing: don't tell me you're not evil!

CREON

If you think mindless, willful stubbornness
is something clever, you're not thinking straight.   550

OEDIPUS

If you think you can harm a family member
and have no punishment, you must be crazy.

CREON

Yes, I agree; what you said then is fair.
But teach me: what's this harm you say you suffered?

OEDIPUS

Did you or did you not persuade me, Creon,
that it was necessary for me to send
someone to fetch that high and mighty prophet?

CREON

Yes, and I still believe that plan was good.

OEDIPUS

So how much time has passed by now since Laius—

CREON

Did what exactly? I don't understand.

OEDIPUS

—vanished, subdued by hands that dealt him death?°   560

CREON

A long and ancient measurement of time.

OEDIPUS

So was this seer not practicing back then?

CREON

Yes, he was just as wise and just as honored.

OEDIPUS

Then at the time, did he name me at all?

CREON

No, at least not when I was standing near him.

OEDIPUS

Did you not have a search to catch the killer?

CREON

Of course we did! But we heard not a thing.

OEDIPUS

Why did this wise man not speak up back then?

CREON

I don't know. When I don't know, I stay silent.

OEDIPUS

You do know this, and you'd be smart to speak!   570

CREON

Of what? If I do know, I won't deny it.

OEDIPUS

That if he hadn't been in league with you
he never would have said that I killed Laius.

CREON

You know if he says that. I think it right
to learn from you, just as you learned from me.°

OEDIPUS

Go on then! But I won't be found a killer!

CREON

All right then. Are you married to my sister?

OEDIPUS

There's no denial possible for that!°

CREON

Do you rule Thebes on equal terms with her?°

OEDIPUS

Yes, I take care of anything she wants.   580

CREON

And am I third, the equal to you two?

OEDIPUS

That's why you're shown up as an evil friend!°

CREON

I'm not! Take time to think, as I have done.
Firstly, consider this: would anyone
prefer to rule accompanied by fear,
than to sleep carefree and have the exact same power?
I, for my part, have no innate desire

to be a leader rather than to lead;
and anybody sane would feel the same.
As things are now, I get it all from you,   590
and never have to fear. But if I were
myself the ruler, I would have to do
many things that I didn't want to do.
So how could I feel happier in power
than having influence at no expense?
I'm not yet so misguided as to want
anything that's not good and beneficial.
As things are now, I can greet everyone,
now everyone is glad to see me, now
people who long for you can call on me,
and they get everything like this, through me.
So why would I lose this to grasp at that?°
I've no desire for those priorities,°
nor would I join another in such actions.
Find proof yourself! Go ask the oracle   600
at Delphi if I've told the truth to you.
And if you catch me plotting with the prophet,
don't kill me by a single vote, but take
a double: yours and mine. Do not accuse me
by unclear evidence, in isolation.°
It is not right to think bad people good
or good ones bad. I say it's just the same   610
if you reject a good and well-loved friend,
or your own life, which you love the most of all.
In time you'll know for certain: only time
reveals an honest man, although you can
recognize someone bad in just one day.

CHORUS (*to* OEDIPUS)
A person careful not to fall, my lord,
would say he's right. Quick thinkers are not stable.°

OEDIPUS
A sly conspirator is plotting fast
against me, so I also must be quick

in planning countermoves. If I sit idle,   620
he'll do what he intends, and I will fail!

CREON
What do you want? To drive me from the land?

OEDIPUS
No, not at all! I want you dead, not exiled.
. . .°

OEDIPUS°
Whenever you reveal what envy is.

CREON°
You mean you will not yield and won't believe me?
. . .°

CREON
I see you can't think straight.

OEDIPUS
                                 I think of me!

CREON
You should be thinking of me too!

OEDIPUS
                                 You traitor!

CREON
If you know nothing . . . ?

OEDIPUS
                         You must still obey me!

CREON
Not if you're ruling badly.

OEDIPUS
City! City!

CREON
I share the city; it's not yours alone.   630

CHORUS
Stop, lords, I see Jocasta coming out
toward you from the house, and right on time;
with her, you should resolve the present quarrel.

(*Enter* JOCASTA, *from the palace.*)

JOCASTA
You idiots! Why did you start to argue?
Aren't you ashamed of picking private fights
during the country's sickness?
                              (*To* OEDIPUS) You go home!
(*To* CREON) And Creon, to your house as well! Don't turn
a trivial problem into something big.

CREON
Sister in blood, your husband Oedipus
imagines that abusing me is right!
He has two terrible ideas: to drive me   640
from my own fatherland, or to seize and kill me!

OEDIPUS
That's right! I caught him, wife, in treachery!
A wicked plot, of physical harm to me!

CREON
No! If I did a single thing you've said,
curse me, and let me die in misery!

JOCASTA
Oedipus! By the gods, believe his words!
Mostly, respect this oath, sworn by the gods,
and also me, and those who stand before you.°

CHORUS°

Sir, I beg you, be willing
to think and to do as they say.

OEDIPUS

What? Why do you want me to yield?   650

CHORUS

Respect him. He's never been stupid,
and now by his oath he is great.

OEDIPUS

Do you know what you want?

CHORUS

                              Yes, I do.

OEDIPUS

                              So then tell me!

CHORUS

For you never to strike at a friend or dishonor his words
when he's under a sanctified curse, and the charge is so
  murky!

OEDIPUS

Then you'd better know, when you're asking for this,
that you're seeking my death or my exile from Thebes.

CHORUS

No, by the god who is chief of all gods,   660
the Sun! May I die the most terrible death,
friendless and godless, if I have that thought!
But our country is dying. This wears at my heart,
and I am so unhappy, if trouble with you two
is about to be added to pain from the past.°

OEDIPUS
Well then, let him go, even if I must die for it—die for it!—
or else be shoved from this country by force, in dishonor.   670
I pity the plight you describe in your words, though
   I don't pity him!
That man will be hated wherever he is!

CREON
It's clear that you hate to give in, and whenever you're far
   gone
in anger, you're cruel. But this kind of character
most hurts the person who has it; it's fair.

OEDIPUS
Now enough! Won't you let me be? Out!

CREON
                                        I will go—
though with no recognition from you. But these men
   know I'm equal.°

(*Exit* CREON, *to the city.*)

CHORUS (*to* JOCASTA, *referring to* OEDIPUS)
Why are you waiting, my lady,
to take this man into the house?

JOCASTA
To find out what happened.   680

CHORUS
Suspicion arose out of words with no knowledge—
but even a false one can bite.

JOCASTA
Were these words from them both?

CHORUS

Yes, they were.

JOCASTA

What was said?

CHORUS

That's enough, in my view. Enough. Let it lie.
It's over. My mind's on our country.

OEDIPUS

You're a sensible man! Do you see what you've come to?
You've loosened and blunted my anger!

CHORUS

Sir, I've said this before, but be sure   690
I'd seem out of my mind, I'd have no brains at all,
if I were abandoning you,
since you brought the fair wind that set my dear country
up straight when it struggled and suffered.
Now guide us to safety.

JOCASTA°

O gods! My lord, whatever was the reason
you roused all this enormous rage? Please tell me!

OEDIPUS

I will; I honor you more highly, wife,   700
than these men.° It was Creon, and his plots!

JOCASTA

Explain your accusation, and this quarrel.

OEDIPUS

He said I am the murderer of Laius!

JOCASTA

Is that his own idea? Did someone tell him?

OEDIPUS
   He sent that wicked prophet in his place;
   he keeps his own mouth free from everything.°

JOCASTA
   Then now you can relax about all this!
   Listen to me, and learn. No mortal being
   has any power at all to tell the future.
   I'll show you instant proof of this. There came   710
   an oracle to Laius once—I'd say
   not from the god himself,° but his attendants—
   that he was doomed to die at his child's hands,
   whatever child he and I had together.
   In fact, the story goes, some foreign robbers
   killed him where three paths meet. Our child was born,
   and only three days later, Laius bound
   his ankles, and with other people's hands
   he hurled him to the mountain wilderness.°
   Apollo did not make that child the killer   720
   of his own father, nor make Laius suffer
   the dreadful death he feared from his own child.
   You need not take the slightest bit of notice
   of things ordained by oracles. A god
   himself will easily reveal his quest.

OEDIPUS
   Wife, as I listened to you speak just now,
   how shaken and distracted was my mind!

JOCASTA
   What worry's overturned you? What do you mean?

OEDIPUS
   It's that I thought I heard you say that Laius
   was murdered at a place where three roads meet.   730

JOCASTA
   That was the story, yes, and it still is!

OEDIPUS

And where is it, the place where this thing happened?

JOCASTA

The land is Phocis, and the forked path leads
to there from Delphi and from Daulia.°

OEDIPUS

And how long is it since these things took place?

JOCASTA

It was announced in town shortly before
you showed up as the leader of our country.

OEDIPUS

O Zeus, what have you planned to do to me?

JOCASTA

What is this, Oedipus, that's on your mind?

OEDIPUS

Don't ask me yet, but tell me about Laius.   740
What did he look like, and what age was he?

JOCASTA

Dark, though he'd started sprouting some white hair;
his build was not dissimilar to yours.

OEDIPUS

Oh no! It seems just now I failed to see
that I was casting curses on myself!

JOCASTA

What's that, my lord? I look at you and tremble.

OEDIPUS

I'm terrified the prophet isn't blind.
But you can clarify: tell one more thing.

JOCASTA
I'll tell you anything, although I'm shaking.

OEDIPUS
Then did he go alone, or bring a large   750
retinue with him, as befits a leader?

JOCASTA
A group of five in all, a bodyguard
among them; Laius traveled in one wagon.°

OEDIPUS
No! Now all this is coming clear.
But wife, who gave you all this information?

JOCASTA
A house-slave. He alone came back alive.

OEDIPUS
Oh! Then is this man in the house right now?

JOCASTA
No. When he came from there and saw that you
were in control, and Laius dead, he begged me,
holding my hand, to send him to the fields   760
and shepherd pastures, very far away
from where the town could see him. And I sent him.
As much as any slave, he did deserve
to have this benefit, and more besides.

OEDIPUS
Then could he get back here to us, and quickly?

JOCASTA
Yes, but for what? Why do you want him to?

OEDIPUS
Wife, I'm afraid that I have said too much,
and that is why I want to see this man.

JOCASTA

Then he will come. But I think that I, too,
deserve to learn why you're upset, my lord.   770

OEDIPUS

You will. I've reached a pitch of dread; who better
to tell than you, when I am in this state?
My mother, Merope, was Dorian;
my father, Polybus, Corinthian.
The citizens back there considered me
important, till this incident that was
surprising, though not worth the fuss I made:
at dinner once, a man had too much wine,
and claimed I was foisted falsely on my father.°   780
I took it hard. That day, I held it in,
but on the next, I went and asked my parents,
and they were very angry at the insult.
And I was glad at their response; but still,
it always gnawed and got to me inside.
Without my parents knowing it, I went
to Delphi, and Apollo sent me back
unsatisfied about the things I asked.
But to my horror, he revealed and told
of other dreadful curses: that I must   790
have sex with my own mother, and produce
children unbearable to human sight,
and be the murderer of my own father.
And when I heard these things, I ran away;
in future, I would mark where Corinth was
by stars,° and go where I might never see
the stigma of those cursed oracles
fulfilled. I traveled, and I reached the place
where you say that this ruler died. And, wife,   800
I'll tell the truth to you. When I had journeyed
near to that triple crossroad, I encountered
a man like you described, with bodyguard,
riding a wagon drawn by colts. The driver,
plus the old man himself, together forced me

off-road. In anger I then struck the driver
who'd made me turn. The old man, seeing this,
watched till I came beside his cart, then hit
my head with a double whip. But he received
a more than equal blow! Briefly: my hand here   810
struck him—I used my stick—and he rolled down
out from the wagon, and then fell down flat.
And so I killed them all. But if there was
some family connection between Laius
and him, this stranger . . . ? What man is worse off
than I am? Who more hated by the gods?
No foreigner or citizen could take me
into their homes, no one can speak to me;
they have to drive me out! And no one else
has cast these curses on me but myself!   820
And by my hands, I taint the dead man's bed:
the hands that killed him. So am I then born bad?
Yes! Am I godless, totally accursed?
Yes! If I have to go away, and, banished,
must never see my people, never set
foot in my fatherland, or I must join
in marriage with my mother, and must kill
my father, Polybus, who fathered me
and brought me up! So wouldn't you
be right to think some cruel god has done this
to me? No, no, I pray the holy gods,   830
may I not ever, ever see the day,
but disappear from human sight, before
I see that taint of fate arrive on me.

CHORUS
This makes us nervous too. But till you hear
from this eyewitness, master, don't lose hope.

OEDIPUS
Yes, this is actually my only hope:
just waiting here for him, the man, the herder.

JOCASTA

What do you want of him when he arrives?

OEDIPUS

I'll tell you. If I find he says the same
as he told you, then I'd be free from trouble.   840

JOCASTA

What in particular from what I said?

OEDIPUS

You said he claimed that robbers, plural, killed him.
If he still says the same in terms of numbers,
I did not kill him, since there is no way
that one man can be equal to a group.
But if he cites a single traveler,
this action then is tipping toward me.

JOCASTA

Yes, that is definitely what he said,
and there's no way that he can take it back.
The city heard all this, not only me.   850
And even if he switched his former story
at all, my lord, he couldn't ever prove
Laius's murder happened as it should have;
Apollo's oracle said he'd be killed
by his and my own son; but that poor boy
died long before; he never murdered Laius.
So after this, I'd never ever spare
a single glance for any oracles.°

OEDIPUS

Good thinking. But in any case, send someone
to get the workman.° Do it, don't forget!   860

JOCASTA

I'll hurry up and do it. Let's go in.
I won't do anything that you won't like.

(*Exeunt* JOCASTA *and* OEDIPUS, *into the palace.*)

CHORUS
  May Fate be with me!
  All my words, all my deeds,
  are holy and reverent!
  Good actions are governed by laws whose feet step high,
  who are born in the heavens above, and Olympus°
  alone is their father. No mortal nature
  poured forth or mothered them.
  Oblivion never will lull them to sleep.
  Great is the god in these places; he does not grow old.   870

  Arrogance fathers sovereignty.° Arrogance,
  if filled too full of too much,
  against what's right and good,
  attains the highest cornices° and then
  topples down headlong to necessity,
  where it can find no footing.
  But I pray to the god not to end
  the wrestling that's good for the city.   880
  I'll never stop having a god as my savior.

  But if someone is using their hands or their words
  to step higher than others,
  and, fearless of Justice,
  shows no due respect to the seats of the gods,
  may evil Fate take them
  to pay back the curse of their pride
  if they profit from ill-gotten gains,
  if they do not hold back from unspeakable words,   890
  if they stupidly touch the untouchable things.
  What man in the midst of such actions could ever
  ward off the weapons of gods from his soul?
  If behavior like this becomes honored,
  then why should I dance in the chorus?°

  No longer will I go to honor the navel
  of earth, the untouchable,

nor to the temple at Abae,   900
nor to Olympia,°
if these things are not tangible truths
fitted fast for all mortals.
Do not forget this, Zeus, master of all!
May your power eternal remember it always.
Indeed, now the oracles told about Laius
are wiped and destroyed
and Apollo is nowhere shown bright in his glory.
Religion is ruined!   910

(*Enter* JOCASTA, *with enslaved attendants, carrying suppliant branches; she addresses the* CHORUS.)

JOCASTA

My lords of Thebes, the thought occurred to me
to come toward the temple with these wreaths
and incense in my arms, since Oedipus
is lifting up his heart too high; he's swayed
by every kind of grief. He does not judge
new facts by old ones, like a man of sense.
He's vulnerable to every word of fear.
I made no progress giving him advice,
so I have come as suppliant to you,
Apollo Lycian, our nearest god,°   920
to pray that you provide us some release
and bless us. As things are, we all are frightened
seeing the pilot of our ship struck down.

(*Enter* FIRST MESSENGER, *from the countryside.*)

FIRST MESSENGER

Strangers, I want to know where I can find
the palace of your ruler, Oedipus.
Please tell me if you know where he may be.

CHORUS

Stranger, this is his house; he is inside.
This is his wife and mother of his children.°

FIRST MESSENGER

I wish her luck and happiness forever,
as Oedipus's true and perfect wife.°   930

JOCASTA

Stranger, the same to you; your kindly words
deserve a blessing. Tell us now why you
have come. What is your news? What do you want?

FIRST MESSENGER

Luck for your home and for your husband, lady.

JOCASTA

But please explain your visit. Who has sent you?

FIRST MESSENGER

I came from Corinth. I'll soon tell my news.
You'll like it, surely, but it might upset you.

JOCASTA

What double power does this message have?

FIRST MESSENGER

The Isthmians° will soon establish him
as ruler there; that's what the people say.   940

JOCASTA

Then is old Polybus no longer ruler?

FIRST MESSENGER

No, he is held inside the grave by death.

JOCASTA

What did you say? That Polybus is dead?°

FIRST MESSENGER

If I am lying, I deserve to die.

JOCASTA (*to one of her enslaved attendants*)
   Slave! To your master, hurry, tell him this!
   Look where you stand now, oracles of gods!
   Years ago, Oedipus was full of fear
   and ran from this man so he would not kill him.
   But now he's dead by chance, not killed by him.

(*Enter* OEDIPUS, *from the palace.*)

OEDIPUS
   My darling wife Jocasta, why have you   950
   called me to come here from inside the house?

JOCASTA
   Listen to this man. As you do, consider
   what those fine holy oracles have come to.

OEDIPUS
   Who is this man? And what's he got to tell me?

JOCASTA
   He's a Corinthian. He came to tell us
   your father, Polybus, is dead and gone.

OEDIPUS
   What is this, stranger? You must be my witness!

FIRST MESSENGER
   If I must first sum up the message clearly,
   know this: the man has gone the way of death.°

OEDIPUS
   Because of treachery? Or some disease?   960

FIRST MESSENGER
   A featherweight tips old limbs down to rest.°

OEDIPUS
   The poor man died of sickness, so it seems.

FIRST MESSENGER
Well, he had measured out a lengthy lifespan.

OEDIPUS
Terrible! Why then, wife, should anyone
consult the hearth of prophecy,° or birds
that cry above us, which foretold that I
would kill my father? Now he's dead and lies
beneath the earth; I'm here; I have not touched
a sword—unless he died of missing me!   970
In that sense, I'm the reason that he died.
So Polybus has taken down to Hades
those oracles, and rendered them worth nothing.

JOCASTA
Did I not tell you all this long ago?

OEDIPUS
You did. But I was led astray by fear.

JOCASTA
So now you need take none of this to heart.

OEDIPUS
How could I not still fear my mother's bed?

JOCASTA
Why should a person fear, when chance rules all,
and nobody has any clear foreknowledge?
It's best to live at random, best you can.
Don't be afraid of marrying your mother.   980
Many a mortal in his dreams has slept
beside his mother. But whoever treats
these things as nothing lives most easily.

OEDIPUS
You would be right in all of this—if only
she were not still alive. But as she is,
I can't be sure if what you say is right.

JOCASTA
Your father's tomb must be an eye of comfort.°

OEDIPUS
Yes, but I am afraid of her, alive.

FIRST MESSENGER
Really? Who is this woman you are scared of?

OEDIPUS
Merope, sir, who lived with Polybus.   990

FIRST MESSENGER
What makes that woman frightening to you?

OEDIPUS
Stranger, the dreadful god-sent oracle.

FIRST MESSENGER
A secret one? Or may a person hear it?

OEDIPUS
You can. Apollo told me I was fated
to have sex with my mother, my own mother,
and shed my father's blood with my own hands.
That's why I have been exiled for so long
from Corinth, my home town. It worked out well,
but still, it's sweet to see one's parents' eyes.

FIRST MESSENGER
What? Did that fear keep you away from Corinth?   1000

OEDIPUS
Yes sir, I did not want to kill my father.

FIRST MESSENGER
Then why, my lord, have I not set you free
from this anxiety? I wish you well.

OEDIPUS
If you did that, you'd get fair recompense.

FIRST MESSENGER
Indeed, that's why I came here: so that when
you came home, I would benefit somehow.

OEDIPUS
I'll never get together with my parents.

FIRST MESSENGER
My child! You clearly don't know what you're doing.

OEDIPUS
What's that, old man? Instruct me, by the gods!

FIRST MESSENGER
If that's the reason that you won't go home   1010

OEDIPUS
I'm scared Apollo's words may turn out true.

FIRST MESSENGER
You're scared of the pollution from your parents?

OEDIPUS
That's it, old man. That fear is always with me.

FIRST MESSENGER
But do you realize you're scared for nothing?

OEDIPUS
How so, if I'm their child, and they my parents?

FIRST MESSENGER
Because he, Polybus, is not your kin!

OEDIPUS
  What do you mean? Did he not father me?

FIRST MESSENGER
  No, he did not! No more than I myself did!   1020

OEDIPUS
  What was his reason, then, to call me "son"?

FIRST MESSENGER
  Listen: he got you as a gift from me.

OEDIPUS
  He loved me—though I came from someone else?

FIRST MESSENGER
  Because before that, he had had no child.

OEDIPUS
  You gave me to him: did you buy or find me?

FIRST MESSENGER
  I found you on the folds of Mount Cithaeron.

OEDIPUS
  Why were you walking in that area?

FIRST MESSENGER
  I was in charge of mountain flocks up there.

OEDIPUS
  You were a homeless man for hire? A shepherd?°

FIRST MESSENGER
  My child, I was your savior at that time.   1030

OEDIPUS
  You picked me up; then what was wrong with me?°

FIRST MESSENGER
Your ankles and your feet could testify.

OEDIPUS
No! What old trouble are you bringing up?

FIRST MESSENGER
Your feet were pierced and I set you free.

OEDIPUS
I brought a dreadful shame out of my cradle.

FIRST MESSENGER
You got your name because this happened to you.°

OEDIPUS
Gods! Did my mother or my father do it?

FIRST MESSENGER
The man I got you from would surely know.

OEDIPUS
So someone gave you me? You didn't find me?

FIRST MESSENGER
Another shepherd handed you to me.   1040

OEDIPUS
Who was it? Could you recognize and show him?

FIRST MESSENGER
I think they called him one of Laius's slaves.

OEDIPUS
You mean the man who used to rule in Thebes?

FIRST MESSENGER
Yes, certainly. This man was that man's herdsman.

OEDIPUS

Is this man still alive? So I could see him?

FIRST MESSENGER

Your Theban countrymen would know that best.

OEDIPUS (*to bystanders and enslaved attendants*)

Does any one of you here know this herder?
The one he mentioned? Have you seen him here,
or in the countryside? If so, speak up!
It's time to find the truth about all this.   1050

CHORUS

I think he means the same man from the country,
the one that you were looking for just now.
Jocasta would be able to explain.°

OEDIPUS

Wife, do you know the man whom recently
we summoned here? Is he the one he means?

JOCASTA

Why mention him? Just turn away, forget
that all these empty words were ever spoken.

OEDIPUS

There's no way I could get such evidence
as this, and not reveal my origins!

JOCASTA

No, by the gods, if you value your life,   1060
don't make this search! My sickness is enough.

OEDIPUS

Don't worry! If I am, on Mother's side,
third-generation slave, you're still a queen!°

JOCASTA

Listen to me, I beg you! Don't do this!

OEDIPUS

No, I won't listen! I must learn the truth.

JOCASTA

I'm saying this with your own good in mind.

OEDIPUS

Then this "own good" has long been harming me.

JOCASTA

You're cursed, poor man. You don't know who
you are.

OEDIPUS

Won't someone go and bring that herdsman here?
Let her enjoy her wealthy family!°   1070

JOCASTA

Oh, you poor man! That's all I have to say,
and it's the last thing that I'll ever say.

(*Exit* JOCASTA.)

CHORUS

Why on earth, Oedipus, has your wife rushed
away, in desperate grief? I am afraid
some trouble will be breaking from her silence.

OEDIPUS

Then let it break! Let her do as she pleases!
But as for me, I want to see the source
of my own birth, however small and lowly.
She's full of pride, as women are, and maybe
she is ashamed of my bad family.°

But I account myself the son of Fate,   1080
who gives good things, and I'll not be ashamed.
She is my mother, and my kindred are
the months that made me small and made me big.
So born, I'd never turn to someone else,
the kind who wouldn't learn my origins.

CHORUS

If I am a prophet
with judgment and knowledge,
I swear by Olympus that you, Mount Cithaeron,
at moonlight tomorrow will be raised up in glory   1090
as ancestor, mother, and nursemaid of Oedipus,
and we will be dancing for you in our chorus
because you bring blessings
for rulers of ours.
Hallelujah, Apollo!°
May this be your will.
But who was your mother, child? Which of the long-lived
nymphs on the mountain had met with your father,
Pan?° Or who slept with Apollo, with Loxias?°   1100
All of the countryside pastures are dear to him.
Or was it Hermes, the lord of Cyllene,
or Bacchus, the god who
inhabits the mountaintops,
who took you as foundling from one of the flashing-eyed
nymphs whom he often
is playing with?°

(*The* HERDSMAN *enters and approaches.*)

OEDIPUS

Gentlemen, I have never met this man,   1110
but if I had to guess, I'd say I see
that herdsman we've been looking for. He matches
this man in his advanced old age, and also
I recognize the men escorting him
as my own house-slaves. But I guess you would
know more than me; you've seen the man before.

CHORUS
Yes certainly, I know him. He served Laius,
an honest man, if any herdsman can be.

OEDIPUS (*to the* FIRST MESSENGER)
I'll ask you first, is this the man you mean,   1120
from Corinth?

FIRST MESSENGER
              Yes, he is the one you see.

OEDIPUS (*to the* HERDSMAN)
Now you, old man, look here and answer all
my questions. Did you once belong to Laius?

HERDSMAN
Yes, not a bought slave; raised up in that house.

OEDIPUS
What was your line of work or way of life?

HERDSMAN
Most of my life was following the herds.

OEDIPUS
And in what places did you mostly shelter?

HERDSMAN
Either Cithaeron or else thereabouts.

OEDIPUS
So did you meet this man there? Do you know him?

HERDSMAN
How would I? Doing what? Who do you mean?

OEDIPUS
This man here. Did you ever interact?   1130

HERDSMAN
  Well, not so I could call to mind right now.

FIRST MESSENGER
  It's not surprising, master. But I will
  remind him. I know well he does remember
  when on Cithaeron's land he drove two flocks
  and I drove one. I was his neighbor
  for three whole six-month seasons, from the spring
  till Arkturus was rising.° Then at winter
  I drove my flocks to my own fold, while he
  drove his to Laius's stables. Am I telling
  the truth or not, in saying all this happened?   1140

HERDSMAN
  You're right, though all of this was long ago.

FIRST MESSENGER
  So come on, tell us, do you know you gave
  a child to me, to bring up as my own?

HERDSMAN
  What is this? Why do you ask about this story?

FIRST MESSENGER (*gesturing to* OEDIPUS)
  This man, my friend, is him. He was that baby.

HERDSMAN
  To hell with you! Why won't you shut your mouth?

OEDIPUS
  Stop that, old man, don't scold him! It is you
  whose words deserve a scolding, not this man.

HERDSMAN
  What wrong have I done, master, best of masters?

OEDIPUS

You failed to speak about the child when questioned.   1150

HERDSMAN

He's talking with no knowledge: futile labor!

OEDIPUS

If you won't talk to help me, pain will make you.

HERDSMAN

No, by the gods, I'm old! Please do not hurt me.

OEDIPUS

Somebody, quickly twist his arms behind him.

HERDSMAN

No, why? Poor me! What do you want to learn?

OEDIPUS

Did you give him the child he asked about?

HERDSMAN

Yes, and I wish I'd died that very day.

OEDIPUS

You'll come to that, if you won't talk as needed.

HERDSMAN

But if I speak, I'm ruined all the more.

OEDIPUS

It seems this man is set on wasting time!   1160

HERDSMAN

I'm not! I said I gave him, long ago.

OEDIPUS

Where did you get him? Your house? Someone else?

HERDSMAN

He wasn't mine. He came from someone else.

OEDIPUS

Which of these citizens? And from which house?

HERDSMAN

No, by the gods, no, master! Ask no more.

OEDIPUS

You're done for if you will not answer me.

HERDSMAN

Well, it was one of the babies born to Laius.°

OEDIPUS

A slave, or born to him as his own kin?

HERDSMAN

I'm on the point of danger in my story—

OEDIPUS

And I in hearing it. But I must hear.   1170

HERDSMAN

They said it was his son. But she, inside,
your wife, would be the best at telling this.

OEDIPUS

Did she give him to you?

HERDSMAN

                    She did, my lord.

OEDIPUS

To do what?

HERDSMAN

So that I might kill the child.

OEDIPUS

Her baby?

HERDSMAN

She was scared of prophecies.

OEDIPUS

What were they?

HERDSMAN

That the child would kill his parents.

OEDIPUS

Then why did you give it to this old man?

HERDSMAN

In pity, master. I thought he could take it
to his own country. But he saved the child
for utmost ruin. And if you are him,   1180
as he says—know that you were born accursed.

OEDIPUS

Oh, oh! Everything now comes clear.
O light, I look at you for the last time!
Now I'm revealed as who I am: the child
of parents who should not have had a child.
I lived with those who should not be together,
and I killed those whom it was wrong to kill.

CHORUS

O generations of mortals,
I count you as equal to nothing,
even when you are alive.
Who indeed, what man, ever wins

more good fortune than just enough   1190
to give an appearance, a show,
then slip down?
You, poor Oedipus, you! I hold the god of your story,°
yours, yours as example,
and I count no mortal happy.

You shot your arrow far beyond°
and mastered good fortune, good blessings,
in everything.
Yes, by Zeus, you destroyed
the girl with the twisted talons
who sang riddling omens!° You stood   1200
against our deaths, as a tower for my land.
From that time onward you were called my king,°
and you have received the greatest of honors,
ruling in this, the greatest of cities,
in Thebes.

But now, who now have you heard of
more deeply unhappy, in troubles more savage,°
who lives with such terrible change in his life?°
O famous, infamous Oedipus!
The same mighty harbor
was enough for both you and your father,
as slaves of the bedroom,
to fall in, the same.°
How on earth could those furrows
—your father's!—how could they
bear you for so long in silence, poor man?°   1210

Time can see everything; time found you out,
though you did not want it. Time brings to justice
your long-ago parented parenting; marriage un-marriage.
Child of Laius,
I wish, how I wish
that I never had seen you.

How intensely I mourn you
and pour from my mouth
a cry of deep grief.° To tell truth,
from you I took breath and through you   1220
I rocked to sleep my eyes.

SECOND MESSENGER (*from the palace*)
Lords, who are always honored in this country,°
I have to tell you, show you, make you feel
such grief—if you are still concerned about
the house of Labdacus, like family.°
No river, I believe—not River Ister
nor Phasis,° with their purity—could wash
this house of all the evil that it holds,
which it will soon be bringing out to light:
deliberate actions, not unwilling ones.°   1230
Self-chosen pains are those that hurt the most.

CHORUS
What we already knew was cause enough
for grieving. What new message are you bringing?

SECOND MESSENGER
The news is very quick to say and quick
to learn: the godlike Queen Jocasta's dead.

CHORUS
Poor woman! Why on earth? What was the cause?

SECOND MESSENGER
She killed herself. You do not have to bear
the worst of it, because you did not see it.
But still, as far as memory can serve,
you'll grasp how terribly the woman suffered.   1240
When she, in fury,° came inside the hall,
at once she dashed toward her marriage bed,
her fingers ripping out her hair. She slammed
the doors shut from the inside, and she called

on Laius, Laius long since dead already,
remembering the seed from long ago
that killed him and left her who gave it birth
with curse of children: children manufactured
by his own children. She cried at the bed,
where she—reduplicated pain!—had borne
husband by husband, children by her child.   1250
How, after that, she died, I do not know.
Oedipus burst in shouting, and he made it
impossible to watch her suffering.
Instead, we looked at him, as he rushed round:
he dashed to ask us for a sword, and where
his wife, not wife, where could he find his mother,
the field of double harvest, of himself
and of his children?° But, as he was raving,
some spirit must have shown him where she was;
it wasn't any of us bystanders.
Screaming terribly, as if he was   1260
guided by someone, at the double doors
he leapt, and from their sockets bent and twisted
those doors, and fell inside the room,° and there
we saw his wife, the woman, hanging from
a twisted noose. And he, when he saw her,
let out a dreadful groan, in misery.
He loosed the rope that she was hanging from;
and once she lay, poor woman, on the ground,
what happened then was terrible to see.
He ripped the spikes of beaten gold she wore
out of her clothing,° and he held them up,
then struck the sockets of his own round eyes,   1270
shouting about how they would not see her,
nor what bad things he did and underwent,
how for the future, they would see in darkness
those he should not have seen; they would not know
those he should not have known. With words like these
he used the spikes to pummel at his eyes,
not once but many times, and as he did so,
his bloody eyeballs drenched his cheeks; they flowed

continually, not ever letting up.°   1280
The former happiness was truly happy,
but now, today: moans, ruin, death, and shame,
whatever evil can be named is here.

CHORUS

Poor man! Has he now found relief from pain?

SECOND MESSENGER

He's yelling, "Someone open up the doors!
Show all the Thebans one who killed his father,
his mother's . . . ." I can't quote those blasphemies.
He said that he would fling himself from Thebes,   1290
not stay, a curse upon the house, as he
himself had prayed. But he is weak and needs
a guide. He is more sick than he can bear.
He'll show you too: the latches of the doors
are opening, and soon you'll see a sight
that even one who hated him would pity.

(*The palace doors open.* OEDIPUS *comes out, his mask altered
to represent his bloody, empty eye sockets.*)

CHORUS°

What terrible pain for a person to see,
most terrible pain I have ever encountered.
What madness, poor man, came upon you? What spirit   1300
leapt further than furthest
onto your spirit-accursed fate?
The sorrow! The pity! My eyes cannot meet yours,
although there's so much that I'd like to be asking you,
so much to learn and so much to look at.
You make me shudder.

OEDIPUS

Oh, oh, oh! I am undone.
What land can I go to? The pity, the pain!
Where are my words being carried? They fly all around.   1310
Spirit, O Spirit!° How far you have leapt!

CHORUS

To horror that cannot be looked at or heard.

OEDIPUS

Darkness! My dark cloud,
attacking, repelling,
not to be spoken of, not to be governed,
blown by a wind of disaster!
Gods, no!
No, again no! What a sting from these sharp points,
what a sting from the terrible memories!

CHORUS

No wonder that in such disaster
you suffer twice over, you feel the pain twice.   1320

OEDIPUS

My friend,
you are still with me, my trusted attendant.
You have stayed to take care of me now I am blind.
Aaah!
I'm not unaware, I can still recognize
your voice through my darkness.

CHORUS

You did terrible things! How could you do it,
to snuff out your eyesight? What spirit inspired you?

OEDIPUS

Apollo, my friends, these things were Apollo,
who brought to fulfillment my pain and my ruin.   1330
But nobody struck me but me: self-handed,
I did it, to my own unhappy self.
Why should I see
when my sight could see nothing joyful?

CHORUS

It was so, as you say.

OEDIPUS

What could I look at and what could I love,
what word could I hear with pleasure, my friends?
Take me away, as fast as you can,   1340
take me, my friends: I am ruin!
I am the most cursed and of all human beings
most hated by gods.

CHORUS

Your mind and your misery—equally pitiful!
How I wish that I had never known you.

OEDIPUS

Damn him, that wandering herdsman, whoever he was,   1350
who took me from that savage bond on my feet
and protected and saved me from death;
he did me no good!
If I had died then I would not be
the cause of such pain to myself and my loved ones.

CHORUS

I wish the same.

OEDIPUS

I would not have come as my own father's killer,
or have people name me the bridegroom
of those I was born from.
Now I am godless, the child of unholy ones,   1360
joint parent with those whose poor child I was.
Now if any ruin outranks any ruin,
it comes to the portion of Oedipus.°

CHORUS°

I don't know how to say your plans were good;
better that you were dead, than living blind.

OEDIPUS

Don't teach me or advise me that my actions

were anything but best. I do not know   1370
how, with what kind of eyes, I ever could
look at my father, when I go to Hades,
or my poor mother. What I've done to them,
those two, deserves much more than death by hanging.
And how could I desire to see the sight
of my own children, given where they came from?
Never, with my own eyes; not ever, ever.
Nor would I see the city or the towers
or holy statues of the gods, from which
I myself banned myself, I who was raised
the one most privileged in Thebes, the one   1380
in total misery: since I myself
declared that everyone must drive away
the one who is unholy, whom the gods
have shown to be unhallowed, from the line
of Laius.° When I had uncovered such
a stain, my stain, would I look with straight gaze
at them? Of course not. If there were some way
to block the stream of hearing through my ears,°
I wouldn't have held back from shutting up
my whole poor ruined body, so I'd be
blind and deaf both. It is sweet to live   1390
inside the mind's house, far away from pain.
O Mount Cithaeron! Why did you take me in?
Why did you not just seize me and destroy me
immediately, so I would never ever
have shown myself to people and revealed
my origins? O Polybus and Corinth,
supposedly my old ancestral home,
you brought me up as if I were so fine,
but I was festering inside. And now
my wrongful nature, wrongful origins,°
have been found out. That place where three roads meet!
That hidden grove, that thicket, narrow place
of triple paths! You drank, from my own hands,   1400
my blood, my father's blood! Do you remember

me? What I did? And what I did next, after
I came here? Marriages! Marriages!° You were
source of my birth, you gave me life, then sent
the same seed back again, and you revealed
fathers as brothers, children, kindred bloodshed,
brides, wives, and mothers, and whatever actions
cause deepest shame among humanity.
What's wrong to do is wrong to speak about.
Hide me outside, as fast as possible,   1410
by gods! Or kill me, or throw me away
into the sea, where you will never see me
ever again. Come on, don't shrink from touching
a miserable man. Do what I say!
Do not be scared. No one, no human being,
could bear my sufferings, but I alone.

(*Enter* CREON, *from the city.*)

CHORUS

Look! Here is Creon, just the man you need
for what you're asking; he can make decisions
and act, since he alone has now been left
as guardian of Thebes,° instead of you.

OEDIPUS

Oh no! How can I answer what he says?
How can I show him that I can be trusted,   1420
when earlier, I treated him so badly?

CREON

No, Oedipus, I did not come to laugh,
nor blame you for bad actions in the past.
But if you can no longer hold in honor
the generations of humanity,
at any rate you should respect the flame
that nourishes all things, our Lord the Sun,
and not display pollution out in public,°
which neither earth, the holy rain, nor light

will find acceptable. (*To his enslaved attendants*) Now
  hurry, quickly!
get him inside the house! It is not holy
for anyone outside the family
to see or hear a family's disasters.   1430

OEDIPUS

By gods, you've far exceeded all my hopes—
the highest man descending to the lowest.
Please do this, for your own sake, not for mine.

CREON

What do you need? What are you asking for?

OEDIPUS

Fling me away, as fast as possible,
out of this land, to somewhere nobody
can speak to me or see me anymore.

CREON

I would have, certainly, if I had not
wanted to find out from god, before all else,
what must be done.

OEDIPUS

                          But what he said already
was totally transparent! That the killer   1440
of his own father, the unholy one,
must die—and that is me.

CREON

                          That's what was said.
But since we stand in such a point of crisis,
it's best to learn from him what must be done.

OEDIPUS

You'll find out, for a wretched man like me?

CREON

Yes, now at last you might trust in the god.

OEDIPUS

I'll lean on you and beg you this: the woman,
bury her as you wish, inside the house—
it's right that you do this for your own people.°
But as for me, let this, my fathers' home,
never be forced to meet me living here;   1450
let me live in the mountains, on my own
Cithaeron, which my mother and my father
appointed for me, living, as my tomb
and caretaker, where I may die a death
caused by the two who have already killed me.
I know this much at least, that I will not
die of disease or any other thing.
I'd never have been saved from death, if not
for terrible disaster of some kind.
But let my fate go anywhere it will!
Creon, you need not worry for my sons,
since they are men, so they will never lack   1460
the means to live, wherever they may be.
But pity my poor daughters! They have never
known me to separate my dinner table
from them; whatever food I touched, they shared.
Please care for them. And most of all, allow me
to touch them with my own hands, and to give them
my cries of grief about our sufferings.
Master, please!°
You're noble in your birth. If I could touch them
with my own hands, it would seem like I had them,
just as I had them back when I could see.   1470
What am I saying?°
Gods, am I really hearing my two darlings
crying? Has Creon pitied me and sent
my dearest, favorite children here to me?
Have I guessed right?

CREON

  Yes, I did this for you; I knew what joy
  they used to give you, and would give you now.

OEDIPUS

  Bless you for bringing them!° And may the spirit
  take better care of you than he did me.
  Children, where are you? Come to me, come here,   1480
  to me—into your brother's arms and hands,
  ambassadors, whose public service° was
  to make your father, your own father's eyes,
  which used to be so clear, see as they do.
  Children, I didn't see, I didn't know,
  but I have been revealed to be your father
  by that same place from which I too was plowed.
  I cannot look at you, but I am crying
  for both of you, considering how bitter
  the life that other people will compel you
  to live will be, from this time going forward.
  What gatherings of citizens will have you?
  What festivals? You will be brought to tears   1490
  and come back home, not see the celebration.
  And when you reach the proper age for marriage—
  children, who will there be, who'd cast his lot
  to get such insults? Names to ruin both
  your parents and you too!° What suffering
  is missing from the list? Your father killed
  his father! And he plowed the one who bore him,
  the place in which he had himself been sown,
  and he got you from sources that were equal
  to where he had come out from his own self.
  This is the kind of insult you'll receive.
  So who will marry you? There's no one, children;   1500
  it's clear, you must be ruined: dry and barren,
  no marriages. Son of Menoeceus,°
  since you alone are left to these two girls
  as father—now that we two who produced them
  are dead and gone—don't let them become homeless,°

husbandless beggars; they're your family.
Pity them! You can see their situation,
with nothing but what you can share with them.
So please say yes, and touch me, trueborn lord!   1510
Children, if you were old enough to listen,
there's so much I would tell you. As it is,
I ask you only this: live as you can.
I pray that you will have a better life
than that of your own father.

CREON
                                   Now enough!
You must stop crying. Go inside the house.

OEDIPUS
I must obey, although it brings no joy.

CREON
Yes, everything is good at its right time.   1520

OEDIPUS
Do you know on what terms I go away?

CREON
You'll tell me and I'll listen. Then I'll know.

OEDIPUS
Send me away in exile from the land.

CREON
You're asking me for what a god must give.

OEDIPUS
But I'm the man most hated by the gods.

CREON
Then you'll soon get it.°

OEDIPUS

Do you mean it?

CREON

Yes.
I don't like saying things I do not mean.

OEDIPUS

Then take me from this place now, right away!

CREON

Go now. But let your children go.

OEDIPUS

No, no!
Don't take these girls from me!

CREON

You must give up
your wish to rule in everything. The power
you had has not stayed with you through your life.

CHORUS

Inhabitants° of Thebes, our fatherland,
look here! This Oedipus, who solved the famous
riddle, and was most powerful, who never
glanced at the citizens' envy, or at fortune,
has now collided with this great tsunami
of ruin. So all mortals ought to look
toward this final day, and call no person
happy, who has not traveled all through life
without experiencing any pain.   1530

Notes

p. 5 orchestra: "Orchestra" literally means "dancing area": the round central area of the Athenian theater used primarily for the chorus. The actors would have been mostly on the raised wooden stage.

p. 5 beside the altar: This and all subsequent stage directions, set in *italics* in the play text, have been added by the translator as a guide to the reader or director; the manuscripts of ancient plays never have stage directions.

p. 5 *Cadmus!*: legendary founder of Thebes, whose name is closely linked to the city.

p. 5 *sitting here*: The word for seat or sitting, *hedra*, occurs in lines 2 and 13 of the Greek text (echoed in this translation by "sitting . . . sitting"; note that this text's line numbers refer to the original Greek). It is a word associated specifically with sitting in supplication or prayer. The emphasis on the suppliants' physical position, sitting down, traces an implicit contrast with Oedipus, the one who is here and, wherever possible, standing on his feet.

p. 5 *they cannot fly yet*: The children are imagined as chicks or fledgling birds.

p. 5 *special acolytes*: They are "special" in that they have been selected, presumably on some kind of merit.

p. 5 *the oracle of ash*: Athena had twin temples at Thebes. The Ismenus was one of the two rivers of Thebes. The "oracle of ash" likely refers to the temple of Apollo, where there was an altar made of the ash from sacrificial victims.

p. 5 *its head / is sunk beneath the deep and bloody waves*: The imagery shifts between the city as a sinking ship and as a single drowning person, whose head is submerged beneath the waves.

p. 6 *Hades*: the god of the dead.

p. 6 *the relentless Poet's tribute*: The "relentless Poet" is the Sphinx, who guarded the entrance to Thebes and killed those who could not solve her riddle as "tribute." Notice that Sophocles does not name the Sphinx and never specifies her riddle. Here, she is referred to by the word commonly used for an oral poetry composer: *aoidos*. The Sphinx is imagined as a kind of poet, whose riddle is a song.

p. 6 *we stood up straight, but then fell down again*: There are repeated metaphors in this first scene of standing and falling, echoed dramaturgically in the position of the seated supplicants, met by the upstanding Oedipus.

p. 6 *Your bird of destiny brought us good luck*: The "bird of destiny" may be any auspicious sign, since birds could stand in for any omen or mark of divine will. But perhaps it is also relevant that the Sphinx is winged.

p. 7 *sick with plague, diseased*: The word *nosos* and its cognate verb *noseo* were used specifically of plague, including the plague of Athens (as Robin Mitchell-Boyask has argued in his *Plague and the Athenian Imagination* [Cambridge, Eng.: Cambridge UP, 2008]); they were also used of mental illness and suffering in general—and of course here there is the dramatic irony that Oedipus is, unknown to himself, "sick" with pollution.

p. 7 *Phoebus*: Apollo, who has the cult title Phoebus, is Artemis's twin brother, the god of the golden bow, and associated with prophecy.

p. 7 CREON *appears from the countryside direction*: In the Athenian theater, the side to the right of the stage was conventionally used to signal exits and entrances toward the countryside; the side to the left was for exits and entrances to the city.

p. 8 *we must expel / pollution . . . not feed it till it turns incurable*: Pollution is a neuter noun in Greek (*miasma*): it is a thing, not a person, but Creon describes it in personified terms, as something that has been taken care of in Thebes, like a child, and may become "incurable," like a deadly disease.

p. 8 *storm of blood*: The metaphor of a "storm of blood" echoes the blood rained down as Zeus's tears in *The Iliad* at the death of Sarpedon (*Iliad* 16.439; cf. 11.53–54); it is caused by the blood shared between Oedipus and his parents, and the spilled blood of Laius.

p. 9 *the selfsame men whose hands killed our dead king*: The term "selfsame" picks up a word in the original, *autoentes*, that is usually used for killing oneself or killing a family member—a "same-killing." Creon uses the plural, as if assuming that more than one person must have been involved in the murder. The question of how many people killed Laius proves essential to the murder mystery and to the themes of the play; see the Introduction.

p. 9 *unless there was / conspiracy in Thebes, and he was bribed?*: Creon insists on the plurality of the attackers, but Oedipus's response assumes there was a single attacker. Oedipus quickly leaps to the idea that there must have been a conspiracy.

p. 10 *Power had fallen*: The Greek also uses the word "fall"; the Greek phrase translated "impediment" (in English, etymologically, a foot-shackle, from Latin *impedimentum*) suggests "bad thing at the feet" *(kakon . . . empodon)*. The word translated "power" is *tyrannis*, "one-person government."

p. 10 *The enigmatic Sphinx made us abandon / puzzles, and look at what was at our feet*: The sentence suggests both that the Sphinx forced the Thebans to focus on the immediate threat she herself posed, and that she made them abandon one riddle (the murder of Laius) in the attempt to solve another (her own, involving numbers of feet).

p. 10 OEDIPUS *remains on stage, listening to the* CHORUS: Oedipus most likely remains on stage during this choral ode; but he may leave and then reenter after the song, making a "powerful re-entrance" (P. J. Finglass, ed. and trans., *Sophocles: Oedipus the King* [Cambridge, Eng.: Cambridge UP, 2018], p. 206).

p. 11 CHORUS: The Chorus members would have been singing and dancing; their words are in a different, much more complex metrical scheme from the main dialogue, as is always the case for choral odes. In this translation, the different meters are reflected by the use of iambic pentameter for dialogue sections (iambic trimeter in the original), and more varied, primarily anapestic rhythms for the choral passages. The first choral ode of a play is called the parodos. Line spaces mark breaks between one metrical unit and the next (called a "strophe" and "antistrophe" in the original, where the music and rhythm of the sections are in a symmetrical pattern).

p. 11 *Artemis, / who sits on the glorious circular throne of the market, / and Phoebus Apollo, far-shooter*: Apollo, who has the cult title Phoebus, is Artemis's twin brother, the god of the golden bow. *Artemis*: It is usually Poseidon, not Artemis, who is responsible for earthquakes. Artemis was known as "glorious" *(eukleia)* in Boeotia; perhaps Sophocles has a specific cult statue of the goddess in mind. The circular throne is appropriate for the goddess of the moon.

p. 11 *no sword of the mind can save us or help us*: This striking metaphor suggests a frustrated hope that mental effort might be able to act as a weapon to save the people of Thebes—as Oedipus's mind did when the city of Thebes was threatened by the Sphinx.

p. 11 *the western god*: Hades is not normally known as the "western god," but the reference must be to him.

p. 11 *children who lie underfoot and bring death*: The ancient Athenians did not know about the exact means by which infectious diseases are spread, but they were certainly aware that the bodies of the sick or dying could cause others to become sick.

p. 12 *piping in harmony*: Synesthetic imagery: the sound of a chant for healing is conveyed by a verb, "shining," normally applied to bright light.

p. 12 *Ares*: the god of war.

p. 12 *Amphitrite*: a sea goddess.

p. 12 *Apollo Lycaios*: Apollo is addressed as Lycaios, a cult epithet that has often been associated with wolves, although the actual meaning of the title is unknown. The title, also used in Jocasta's prayer later in the play (line 919 in the

Greek text), may be associated with Apollo's role as cause and healer of disease. There was a temple and cult of Apollo on Mount Lycaion, a remote, rocky area.

p. 12 *Bacchus*: = Dionysos, who is "named after Thebes" because one of his cult titles was "Cadmean" (*kadmeios*), in allusion to his Theban heritage, as the son of the Theban princess Semele. Dionysos was traditionally accompanied by wildly ecstatic women dressed in furs, called maenads (the mad women). The "whoop" of the maenads is their traditional ecstatic cry, often rendered with the onomatopoeic word "euhoe!"

p. 12 *the god whom the gods are ashamed of*: The other gods are (according to the Chorus) ashamed of Ares, as god of destruction.

p. 12 *I am a foreigner to this event, / and unfamiliar with what was said*: Oedipus applies to himself the word *xenos*, meaning "stranger," "guest," or "noncitizen": as a person from a different city-state, he was a *xenos* in Thebes, and also—he suggests—a metaphorical "stranger" in terms of being informed about the killing of Laius.

p. 13 *without a clue*: The Greek is ambiguous. It could suggest, "If I had been able to investigate right away, I would have found a clue long ago." Or it could be, "I would not have got far with the investigation, if there was no clue." The ambiguity underlines the crucial question of whether there is already evidence available to Oedipus that he could in theory "track."

p. 13 *if the killer / is scared to blame himself*: There may be a lacuna (gap in the text) between lines 227 and 228, with a line missing that said something like, "the killer need not be [afraid of blaming himself]."

p. 13 *if someone / knows that the killer came from somewhere else*: Oedipus fits all the possibilities he outlines: he is a Theban and a man from a different city.

p. 13 *I will make sure that man / receives his proper thanks and due reward*: more dramatic irony, since Oedipus will give himself his due reward for revealing the truth.

p. 13 *the holy water*: The "holy water," *chernips*, is water used for purification of a crowd of worshippers; it was made holy by dipping a brand heated at the altar of sacrifice into the water. Oedipus is ordering that the murderer suffer the ancient equivalent of excommunication: he will be excluded from all types of religious ceremonies.

p. 13 *the Pythian oracle*: at Delphi.

p. 13 *Whether the secret criminal did this / alone or with accomplices, I pray / that he wears out a poor, unlucky life / in misery*: This sentence may be interpolated from an actor's emendation of the text; see Finglass, *Oedipus the King*, p. 252.

p. 14 *and sow his wife / with him*: Literally, the wife is described as "together-sown," *homosporos*.

p. 14 *we would have common children*: Again, dramatic irony: Oedipus thinks Laius had bad luck in that he had no children; but we know that his bad luck as a father was different. "Common children" suggests, for Oedipus, "children who shared a mother," i.e., half-siblings.

p. 14 *Fate has leapt upon his head*: Fate (*Tyche*) is personified and imagined as jumping onto Laius.

p. 14 *the selfsame man whose own hands killed the son*: The original uses *auto-cheir*, literally, "same-hand," which can connote a suicide, or a person who achieves something with his or her own hands, or a person who kills a family member. Oedipus uses the word to denote the murderer, who killed Laius with his own hands; but the connotation of "family-killer" or "self-killer" adds yet more dramatic irony.

p. 14 *offspring of Agenor / in ancient times*: The patrilinear genealogy shows Oedipus demonstrating what he imagines is firm knowledge of Laius's family and paying homage to a line that he imagines has been wiped out. Agenor is the mythical father of Cadmus.

p. 15 *investigation in these things / would gain most clear enlightenment from him*: The Chorus repeats the word for "Lord" (*anax*) three times. The language of sight and seeing runs through the Tiresias scene, as here: "excels / at seeing" (*skopon*) and "most clear enlightenment" (*ekmathoi saphestata*: literally, "from whom one may learn most clearly").

p. 15 *I have already worked this field as well*: Oedipus says he has not acted "in fallow fields," *en argois*.

p. 16 *If you have information from the birds*: It was traditional for diviners in antiquity to interpret the flight and behavior of birds as a sign of the gods' will.

p. 17 *I will never / reveal my ruin: I will not say "yours"*: Tiresias is speaking in deliberately riddling language, not revealing what or whose the "ruin" is.

p. 17 *You criticize my temperament, and blame me; / you do not know the one you're living with*: There is a double meaning: Oedipus does not know the temperament or character or rage he lives with, but also does not know the "one" he lives with, i.e., Jocasta. In the Greek, "temperament," "character," or "anger," *orgē*, is a feminine noun; Tiresias says, "You do not know the [feminine] one you live with." The word *orgē* is picked up in Oedipus's response, when he asks who would not "lose his temper" (*orgizoito*).

p. 18 *The truth I raise is powerful*: Tiresias here uses an essential repeated verb in the play, *trepho*, "to raise up"—used for the raising of children or plants, and here, by extension, of Tiresias's metaphorical child: truth.

p. 18 *Is this a test?*: The text of this phrase is uncertain. The manuscript reading, *e kpreirae legein*, suggests, "Or are you trying to speak?" which makes little sense; probably "to speak" has been substituted for a different original word. The general sense—"Are you testing me?" or "Are you trying to trick me?"—seems clear.

p. 18 *I say you are the murderer you seek*: The text reads more literally, "I say you are the killer of the man whom you seek," a syntactical elision suggesting, on the face of it, that Oedipus is looking for Laius.

p. 20 *my friend right from the first*: Creon is described using a phrase that suggests "my friend from the beginning," but could also suggest "my friend motivated by power": the same word, *arche*, can mean "power" or "beginning."

p. 20 *that song-composer*: The Sphinx, still unnamed, is described as a *rhapsoidos*, which connotes literally a "song-stitcher": a person who performed selections of the Homeric poems and other traditional narrative poetry, with musical accompaniment. It is very unusual to see the word with the feminine article;

real human rhapsodes were usually men. The Sphinx was the daughter of the Chimera (a goat-lion creature) and the dog Orthos, and niece of the three-headed guard dog of the underworld, Cerberus.

p. 21 *Creon's list of immigrants*: The language in the original suggests an allusion to the Athenian law whereby magistrates (*prostatai*) had to register all legal immigrants (*metoikoi*). Tiresias is insisting that he is a native of Thebes and not under the patronage of Creon.

p. 23 *an intmigrant, noncitizen*: The sequence of binary contrasts begins with a contrast between an immigrant permanent resident (a "metic") and a citizen.

p. 23 *his fortune*: Fortune, *symphora*, could be either good or bad luck.

p. 23 *Who did the things unspeakable, unspeakable, / with bloody hands of murder?*: The Chorus members have almost blind faith in Oedipus and Tiresias, and can initially make no sense of what they have witnessed.

p. 23 *the bull*: The murderer is described as a "bull" because he is like a sacrificial animal.

p. 23 *the earth's navel*: Delphi, imagined as the center of the world's body.

p. 24 *I don't know now . . . in solving their mystery deaths*: The Chorus members use obscure language to avoid spelling out the dangerous possibility that they are hinting at: that their own powerful and well-respected leader, Oedipus, might be responsible for the death of Laius. They hedge by several means: emphasizing Oedipus's good reputation; using metaphor (the "evidence" is described in the original as a "touchstone"—a stone used to test the quality of a metal); avoiding the name of Laius (referred to in the plural as "the sons of Labdacus"); and pluralizing a singular event and singular victim (the "deaths" of the "Labdacids," or sons of Labdacus, rather than the single murder of Laius— the Chorus members are still unaware that Oedipus, too, is a Labdacid). All this deliberate obscurity marks the Chorus's awareness of how dangerous it would be to accuse the supreme leader of Thebes of murdering his predecessor. The lines are also textually corrupt, and a word or phrase is missing.

p. 24 *A man may surpass / wisdom by wisdom*: Another mysterious, carefully veiled utterance: the Chorus has half-questioned whether Tiresias is right, then acknowledges that there can be distinctions in human wisdom, then reiterates a skeptical position.

p. 25 *But he himself is coming outside now*: This line is likely an interpolation (put into the text by someone after Sophocles).

p. 27 *subdued by hands that dealt him death?*: The original uses *cheiroma*, meaning literally "handing," or metaphorically "overpowering."

p. 28 *I think it right / to learn from you, just as you learned from me*: I.e., Creon hopes to question Oedipus, as Oedipus has just questioned Creon. Creon implies ignorance of what Tiresias has said.

p. 28 *There's no denial possible for that!*: Oedipus treats the question as a joke, although later in the play he will wish he could deny the marriage.

p. 28 *Do you rule Thebes on equal terms with her?*: It is unclear whether this question implies a formal or legal division of power equally between Oedipus and Jocasta, and possibly Creon too, or a more informal arrangement by which

Oedipus allows Jocasta primary influence over his decisions, rather than an official sharing of power. Oedipus's reply maintains the ambiguity: it could suggest an indulgent husband fulfilling his wife's whims, or it could suggest a more equal sharing of power. This point is important, since if Oedipus is not in fact the sole ruler of Thebes, he is not actually a *tyrannos*, a term that implies one-person rule. There is a real question about whether the city is a tyranny or an oligarchy.

p. 28 *an evil friend*: The word for "friend," *philos*, also implies family member.

p. 29 *So why would I lose this to grasp at that?*: The translation here omits a line that makes little sense (line 600 in the Greek text), which is presumably a corrupt addition, an irrelevant quotation written in the margin of somebody's edition that made its way into the received text. It reads something like, "No evil mind could turn to thinking well."

p. 29 *I've no desire for those priorities*: Creon describes himself as not being a "desirer" or "lover," using a word (*erastes*) that could have erotic connotations (as in an older man's desire for an adolescent boy), but could also be less clearly sexual. Some editors have thought there might be a gap in the text, since it is odd to have a desire for "priorities," or a "view" or "opinion," rather than for the content of the opinion. If the text is correct, this is presumably a highly condensed and poetic way of saying, "I don't want to be the kind of person who thinks being in a prominent leadership position is worth it."

p. 29 *in isolation*: This suggests either "by yourself" (repeating the previous line) or "in isolation from the facts."

p. 29 *Quick thinkers are not stable*: The Chorus gives an allusive, periphrastic, and metaphorical commendation of Creon's speech, avoiding giving Oedipus a direct warning that he might be in trouble.

p. 30 . . . : Here there seems to be a gap of some lines that have fallen out of the received text, since the following line does not make sense as a response.

p. 30 OEDIPUS: The manuscripts ascribe this line to Creon, but some scholars argue persuasively that it really belongs to Oedipus, since Oedipus is the one obsessed with envy.

p. 30 CREON: This line is ascribed to Oedipus by the manuscripts, but again it is more likely to belong to Creon, since Oedipus is the one, in this scene and consistently in the play, who is urged to yield and be persuaded.

p. 30 . . . : Another line at least seems to be missing here; we would expect Oedipus to speak at least one more line before Creon speaks again (as is the norm in stichomythic dialogue, when characters exchange lines). Creon's next half-line seems like a response to Oedipus's having made some further iteration of his obstinacy.

p. 31 *respect this oath, sworn by the gods, / and also me, and those who stand before you*: Jocasta seems to take Creon's utterance as an oath by the gods, although he has not mentioned the gods explicitly. "Those who stand before you" are presumably the Chorus members.

p. 32 CHORUS: The meter now shifts to lyric, a mark of high emotional tension. The original includes a lot of dochmiac rhythms, suggesting urgency.

p. 32 *pain from the past*: This vague phrase could imply pain that actually is past (the Sphinx's tribute), or pain that has been going on for a while (the plague).

p. 33 *I will go— / though with no recognition from you. But these men know I'm equal*: The original for "no recognition" suggests literally that Creon is "unknown" by Oedipus (important in a play so focused on different kinds of knowledge); the word *agnotos* could also mean "ignorant" or "harsh." The word translated "equal," *isos*, can mean "fair" or "impartial." The scholiasts (ancient commentators) suggest that the sentence means, "These men know that I am the same as I was before." For the interpretation of the line given here (*isos* = "good" or "just"), see the discussion in Finglass, *Oedipus the King*, pp. 383–84.

p. 34 *JOCASTA*: The meter now switches back to normal iambic dialogue, in the original as in the translation.

p. 34 *these men*: the Chorus members.

p. 35 *he keeps his own mouth free from everything*: The metaphor by which Creon keeps his mouth "free" is unusual, since a "free" mouth or "free" speech, in ancient Greek as in modern English, usually suggests openly talking about illicit subjects rather than the opposite. Oedipus seems to mean that Creon keeps his mouth free from dangerous and blameworthy utterances.

p. 35 *the god himself*: Below the god is specified as Phoebus (Apollo).

p. 35 *with other people's hands / he hurled him to the mountain wilderness*: The phrasing makes Laius active, although not with his own hands.

p. 36 *The land is Phocis, and the forked path leads / to there from Delphi and from Daulia*: Phocis is the region in Greece that includes Delphi. The third road of the three is to or from Thebes, to the east. Delphi is the home of Apollo's oracle, to the west; Daulia, to the north, was on the edge of Boeotia.

p. 37 *A group of five in all, a bodyguard / among them; Laius traveled in one wagon*: There are one driver; one bodyguard (a more high-ranking attendant); and two enslaved attendants, who are perhaps walking, not riding in the wagon.

p. 38 *I was foisted falsely on my father*: The suggestion might be that Oedipus was the son of another woman, not Merope—or that he was her son by another man.

p. 38 *in future, I would mark where Corinth was / by stars*: The wording is difficult here. The received text, *ekmetroumenos*, suggests that Oedipus plans to measure out the area of Corinth like a surveyor, which is an odd use of language. The emendation *tekmaroumenos* suggests rather that he is "judging," "figuring," or "estimating" the location, by the stars. The manuscript reading may be correct, since this play includes a great deal of language involving measurement, and Sophocles sometimes uses language in obscure metaphorical ways. I have translated the emended text, which is easier to understand.

p. 40 *I'd never ever spare / a single glance for any oracles*: This odd phrase (to "spare a glance," or "look this way or that") is unparalleled in other extant texts and may be a deliberately strange coinage or an unknown idiom. It clearly suggests not caring (about oracles), but the suggestion of sight ties in with the play's obsessive focus on eyes and seeing; Jocasta expresses a deliberate refusal to look in a certain direction.

p. 40 *workman*: This man is described with a number of different terms: as "workman" (*ergates*) here, and also as an "enslaved person" and messenger.

p. 41 *Olympus*: mountain imagined to be the home of the most powerful gods.

p. 41 *Arrogance fathers sovereignty*: This famous line is much debated by scholars. Some argue it should be emended to read, "The tyrant fathers arrogance," but there is no clear reason to accept the suggestion, and the flow of thought and sound works better the other way. The word translated "arrogance" is *hybris*, which suggests any kind of violence or overstepping of natural boundaries. Tyrant, *tyrannos*, is a neutral term elsewhere in Sophocles, but is sometimes used negatively by other authors in this period. The word translated "fathers," *phuteuei*, could suggest either animal or human or plant growth. Here, as throughout the ode, it is unclear whether the Chorus is referring directly to Oedipus (and questioning his legitimacy and his piety) or making vague generalizations.

p. 41 *attains the highest cornices*: The text here is doubtful, and "cornices" is an emendation proposed because the received text is metrically wrong; the word for "cornice," *geisa*, is unusual, so might have been missed by scribes. The image suggests someone making a strange ascent up a high and elaborately decorated building—perhaps the backdrop of the stage, the front of the palace, was painted as if with cornices on the roof. Aristotle in the *Poetics* says that Sophocles was the first tragedian to use painted scenery.

p. 41 *then why should I dance in the chorus?*: This seems to be a metadramatic moment: the Chorus members are asking why they should participate in this tragic chorus, which is part of a religious ritual in honor of the god Dionysos, if those who act impiously can get away with it, and even accrue honor.

p. 42 *nor to the temple at Abae, / nor to Olympia*: Abae also had a sanctuary of Apollo. There was a temple to Zeus at Olympia; Olympia was also, like Delphi, a center for prophecy.

p. 42 *Apollo Lycian, our nearest god*: Apollo is the nearest god both because his altar is in front of the palace, and because he is most closely associated with oracles and prophecies. On "Lycian" see the note to p. 12 above.

p. 42 *This is his wife and mother of his children*: A momentary double entendre, since Jocasta is Oedipus's wife and mother *tout court*, as well as his wife and the mother of his children.

p. 43 *Oedipus's true and perfect wife*: The First Messenger may be implying Jocasta is truly his wife because she has his children; marriages were imagined to be sealed by offspring.

p. 43 *The Isthmians*: Corinth was built on an isthmus, so the Isthmians are the Corinthians.

p. 43 *What did you say? That Polybus is dead?*: A couple of words are missing from this line in the original.

p. 44 *the man has gone the way of death*: Despite claiming a desire to speak clearly, the First Messenger uses notably convoluted language, perhaps in his desire not to cause grief or offense that might be dangerous for him.

p. 44 *A featherweight tips old limbs down to rest*: There is an implicit metaphor of scales weighing the difference between life and death; this scale tips easily for those who are very old.

p. 45 *the hearth of prophecy*: Delphi is imagined as the hearth of the world since it is supposedly at the center of the earth.

p. 46 *an eye of comfort*: literally, "a great eye." The word "eye" is used in Greek as an endearment, as we might call somebody the "apple of my eye." But the usage here is unparalleled in extant Greek: it is never used of a tomb rather than of a living person.

p. 48 *You were a homeless man for hire? A shepherd?*: Oedipus's question suggests a snobbish contempt for the First Messenger's lowly station, which is corrected by the response.

p. 48 *You picked me up; then what was wrong with me?*: Oedipus assumes that the First Messenger must have saved him from some physical ailment.

p. 49 *You got your name because this happened to you*: The name "Oedipus" could suggest either "Know-Foot" (from the verb *oida*, "know," and *pous*, "foot") or "Swell-Foot" (from the verb *oideo*, "to swell"). The Messenger is suggesting the latter etymology. See Introduction, p. viii.

p. 50 *Jocasta would be able to explain*: It is not explained how the Chorus would know this.

p. 50 *If I am, on Mother's side, / third-generation slave, you're still a queen!*: A third-generation slave means one whose grandparent was enslaved. Oedipus assumes that Jocasta is worried he will turn out to have slave heritage.

p. 51 *Let her enjoy her wealthy family!*: Oedipus assumes that Jocasta, who comes from a rich royal household, is motivated by snobbery, rejecting him because, as an exposed foundling child, he may be the son of enslaved or poor people.

p. 51 *bad family*: There is irony in Oedipus using the phrase "bad family" (*dusgeneia*, literally, "bad birthing").

p. 52 *Hallelujah, Apollo!*: The Greek cry is *ie*, an exclamation to a god used in times of extreme emotion; it formed an epithet for the god, as here, so that Apollo is addressed as *ieie*, a god to whom we call *ie*.

p. 52 *Pan*: a god of wild places and the countryside. Nymphs are goddesses closely associated with wild places, either mountains, waters, caves, or trees.

p. 52 *Loxias*: a cult title of Apollo, associated with his role as provider of oracles. The Chorus imagines that Apollo might be the father of Oedipus, by some unknown mother.

p. 52 *Or was it Hermes . . . whom he often / is playing with?*: Hermes is another god associated with the countryside and with ambiguous signs; he was born on Mount Cyllene in Arcadia. Bacchus = Dionysos (see note to p. 12 above), another god of the wild associated with the nymphs. The word translated "flashing-eyed" is written in most manuscripts as "Heliconian" (*Helikonidon*), as if suggesting that these nymphs come from a different mountain; but this reading is unmetrical, and it is strange to associate the nymphs with a different mountain from the one on which Oedipus was abandoned.

p. 54 *from the spring / till Arkturus was rising*: A line is missing in this sentence. The Bear-Watcher, Arkturus, is the brightest star in the constellation Boöetes; its rise marks the beginning of winter in this region.

- **p. 56** *it was one of the babies born to Laius*: The phrasing could cover both those born biologically to Laius and those born to people enslaved in Laius's household and, hence, his property.
- **p. 58** *god of your story*: This phrase in the original is *daimon*: literally, a divine force or deity that controls individual destinies. The word translated "good fortune" in line 1190 is cognate, *eudaimonia*: it suggests a life blessed throughout by a benevolent deity.
- **p. 58** *You shot your arrow far beyond*: The image of Oedipus as a far-shooting archer, who "shot" successfully in solving the riddle of the Sphinx, associates the mortal man with the god Apollo, who is frequently given the epithet "far-shooting" (see note to p. 11 above). There is a momentary hint that Oedipus may have shot not just superlatively far, but perhaps too far.
- **p. 58** *the girl with the twisted talons / who sang riddling omens!*: As usual in this play, the Chorus avoids mentioning the Sphinx by name; she is herself a riddle.
- **p. 58** *you were called my king*: "King" in Greek is *basileus*, a word that, as noted in the Introduction (p. x), seems to contradict Oedipus's self-presentation as a *tyrannos*, a nonhereditary monarch. Bernard Knox ("Why Is Oedipus called *Tyrannos*?" *Classical Journal* 50.3 [December 1954]: 97–102) suggests that the term is used here because now the Chorus members realize that their ruler is in fact the heir to the throne by kinship. Others argue that the various political terms are not so sharply distinguished.
- **p. 58** *in troubles more savage*: The language of wildness or savagery (*agrios*) marks the way that Oedipus's geographical and social position has changed, from being at the center and pinnacle of social life in the city to being an outcast, to a world beyond cultivated fields, in the mountains and deserts and uninhabited areas of earth.
- **p. 58** *who lives with such terrible change in his life?*: The text of line 1205 is corrupt. My translation is based on the tentative suggestion of Finglass following Kassel (Finglass, *Oedipus the King*, p. 533).
- **p. 58** *The same mighty harbor . . . to fall in, the same*: Jocasta's vagina or womb is the metaphorical harbor into which both father and son have sailed or "fallen"; falling on or into is a common metaphor for sex. The word translated "slave of the bedroom," *thalamepolos*, literally, "bedroom-server," is a standard term for a female domestic attendant or enslaved woman in Homer, and it can also be used for male eunuchs. Here the word is usually explained as meaning "bridegroom," but this usage would be entirely unparalleled. Sophocles is more likely making a striking extension of a word usually applied to low-class or enslaved people to apply to the elite Laius and Oedipus in their bedroom service.
- **p. 58** *How on earth could those furrows . . . bear you for so long in silence, poor man?*: The metaphor switches so that Jocasta's body is now a plowed field, whose "furrows" have been sown by both father and son.
- **p. 59** *a cry of deep grief*: The text here is corrupt; I follow the text as printed in Finglass, *Oedipus the King*.

p. 59 *Lords, who are always honored in this country*: The Chorus members, the old elite of Thebans, are now almost the default rulers, because the royal family is destroyed.

p. 59 *like family*: The text is debated. The word translated "like family," *engenos*, is taken by the ancient commentators (the scholiasts) to be metaphorical, connoting "truly," like a true-born child. The word is emended by some scholars to *eugenos*, "nobly," on the grounds that the Chorus members are not actually part of Oedipus's family. I have kept the manuscript reading, because Sophocles is very likely playing on what it means to act in a familial way, in accordance with birth or *genos*, and exploring the muddled distinction between Oedipus's birth family and his ostensibly adoptive Theban family.

p. 59 *not River Ister / nor Phasis*: The Ister is the ancient name for the Danube; the Phasis is the modern-day Rioni.

p. 59 *deliberate actions, not unwilling ones*: The line insists on a distinction between the earlier parricide/incest and the more recent deliberate self-blinding.

p. 59 *in fury*: The word *orgē* is applied earlier to Jocasta in a play on words by Tiresias (see note to p. 17 above). Commentators and dictionaries claim that this word is here being used in a unique sense, unparalleled in extant Greek, to mean "passion" rather than "fury," apparently because most commentators are unable to imagine why Jocasta might be angry. But the text says that she is angry, and she has good reason to be so, given that her whole life has been ruined. Whereas the central object of Oedipus's violent rage turns on his own perceptions (his eyes) and the god Apollo, Jocasta's rage centers on her marriage and her marriage bed, the locus of elite female status.

p. 60 *he dashed to ask us for a sword . . . and of his children?*: The Messenger treats Oedipus's words partway between quoted and indirect speech.

p. 60 *at the double doors / he leapt . . . and fell inside the room*: These concrete details suggest an echo between the woman inside the room and the room itself; she, like it, has a "double" entry, in that she has been penetrated by both father and son; Oedipus has "fallen" into her before.

p. 60 *He ripped the spikes of beaten gold she wore / out of her clothing*: Elite Greek women usually wore an ankle-length gown, a *chiton*, fastened at the shoulders with two long spikes, *fibulae*. I have used the word "spike" rather than "brooch" or "pin," because *fibulae* were often long, substantial pieces of sharpened metal. Designed to be strong enough to hold up a heavy weight of cloth, they were sturdy enough to pierce through the eyeball.

p. 61 *her bloody eyeballs drenched his cheeks; they flowed / continually, not ever letting up*: The translation here omits four lines that are likely interpolated, since they are full of metrical and linguistic problems. The lines read: "The dripping globs of gore; and with all that / black rain of hail, of blood, was being wetted. / These evils broke from two, not one; they came / commingled suffering, for man and woman."

p. 61 CHORUS: The meter shifts to lyric.

p. 61 *Spirit, O Spirit!*: In the original, the "Spirit" is *daimon*, an unspecified divine force.

p. 63 *Now if any ruin outranks any ruin, / it comes to the portion of Oedipus*: Oedipus suggests that the most "outranking" or "more senior" (*presbuteron*) trouble or ruin belongs to him, and has come to him by lot (*elache*), like many political offices in classical Athens. He imagines his situation as an elevation to the top ranks of pollution.

p. 63 CHORUS: The meter switches back to regular iambic here.

p. 64 *the one who is unholy . . . from the line / of Laius*: The gods have revealed the paradox, that the polluted man comes from the royal family.

p. 64 *to block the stream of hearing through my ears*: The orifices of the body are the "doors" by which the public world impinges on the private self.

p. 64 *wrongful origins*: The word for "wrongful" or "bad," *kakos*, can also connote lower-class.

p. 65 *Marriages! Marriages!*: The original is plural; this could be plural standing in for singular, or it could refer to Jocasta's two marriages, or it could be that Oedipus is imagining his marriage as inherently plural (generative of plural, mixed, incestuous family roles).

p. 65 *guardian of Thebes*: The Chorus characterizes Creon not as the monarch or ruler or sovereign (not *tyrannos* or *basileus*), but as "guardian," *phylax*, as if he occupies a caretaking role.

p. 65 *and not display pollution out in public*: Creon contradicts Oedipus's claim that he can touch anybody, since the burden of his sufferings is borne by him alone; according to Creon, Oedipus is tainted by deadly pollution, and should hide himself from the natural and divine as well as human worlds.

p. 67 *it's right that you do this for your own people*: Jocasta, Creon's sister, is still part of his family; Oedipus, an in-law by a tainted, unholy marriage, is not.

p. 67 *Master, please!*: This is a short (one-foot) line in the original, marking the intense emotion.

p. 67 *What am I saying?*: Another short line in the original, again only a third of normal metrical length.

p. 68 *Bless you for bringing them!*: literally, "for this road," an idiomatic way of expressing any arrival or trip, but with an extra resonance in a play where roads and crossroads have been so significant.

p. 68 *into your brother's arms and hands, / ambassadors, whose public service*: The odd language by which hands are "ambassadors" echoes the original verb, *prouxenesan* (*proxeno*), which literally connotes a person performing the office of a *proxenos*, a visiting dignitary from another city who is a public guest and friend of the state. The verb can be used to signify simply "perform" or "do," but the metaphor may be alive; Oedipus imagines his own hands and other body parts as separate people. As Finglass notes (*Oedipus the King*, p. 55), there may also be "a particular irony" in the image, since Oedipus has moved so disastrously from one city to another. The earlier image, by which the body is a house, has now given way to a different image, by which the body is a conglomeration of people inhabiting different city-states.

p. 68 *Names to ruin both / your parents and you too!*: The text in this sentence is problematic; I have rendered what seems to be the general sense.

p. 68 *Son of Menoeceus*: Creon.

p. 68 *are dead and gone—don't let them become homeless*: The text of this line is problematic; the transmitted text is unmetrical, and the verb as translated here ("let them") is a guess.

p. 69 *Then you'll soon get it*: i.e., the gift of exile.

p. 70 *Inhabitants*: These last lines are probably not by Sophocles but by a later interpolator, because they are riddled with linguistic difficulties; see further discussion in Finglass, *Oedipus the King*, 615–17. Some commentators have also objected on the grounds that the sentiments expressed here are hokey, although simplistic moralizing is fairly common at the end of Athenian tragedy.

Further Reading

There are two good recent collections of essays in English on Sophocles: the Brill *Companion to Sophocles*, edited by Andreas Markantonatos (2012), and the Wiley-Blackwell *Companion to Sophocles*, edited by Kirk Ormand (2012). There is also a recent *Brill's Companion to the Reception of Sophocles* (2017). Good single-author introductions to Sophocles include:

A. F. Garvie, *The Plays of Sophocles*, 2nd ed. (London and New York: Bloomsbury, 2016).

Jacques Jouanna, *Sophocles: A Study of His Theater in Its Political and Social Context* (Princeton, NJ: Princeton UP, 2018). Translated from the French.

James Morwood, *The Tragedies of Sophocles* (Bristol, Eng.: Bristol Phoenix Press, 2008).

Charles Segal, *Sophocles' Tragic World* (Cambridge, MA: Harvard UP, 1995).

The recent edition of the Greek text by P. J. Finglass (Cambridge, Eng.: Cambridge UP, 2018) has voluminous notes, many of which can be understood without knowledge of Greek. For discussion of the Oedipus plays from a philosophical perspective, see the recent collection *The Oedipus Plays of Sophocles: Philosophical Perspectives*, edited by Paul Woodruff (Oxford, Eng.: Oxford UP, 2018). On the Oedipus myth beyond Sophocles, see:

J. N. Bremmer, "Oedipus and the Greek Oedipus Complex." In *Interpretations of Greek Mythology*, ed. J. N. Bremmer (London: Croom Helm, 1987), pp. 41–59.

Ettore Cigano, "Oedipodea." In *The Greek Epic Cycle and Its Ancient Reception: A Companion*, ed. Marco Fantuzzi and Christos Tsagalis (Cambridge, Eng.: Cambridge UP, 2015), pp. 213–25.

Lowell Edmunds, *Oedipus* (London and New York: Routledge, 2006).

A good general introduction to the themes of the play can be found in Charles Segal, *"Oedipus Tyrannus": Tragic Heroism and the Limits of Knowledge* (Oxford, Eng.: Oxford UP, 2001). The following books and articles are recommended for discussion of more specific issues and particular scenes:

Allan, William. "'Archaic' Guilt in Sophocles' *Oedipus Tyrannus* and *Oedipus at Colonus*." In *Tragedy and Archaic Greek Thought*, ed. Douglas L. Cairns. Swansea: Classical Press of Wales, 2013, pp. 173–91.

Bain, David. "A Misunderstood Scene in Sophokles, *Oidipous* (*O.T.* 300–462)." *Greece & Rome* 26.2 (October 1979): 132–45.

Budelmann, Felix. "The Mediated Ending of Sophocles' *Oedipus Tyrannus*." *Materiali e discussioni per l'analisi dei testi classici* 57 (2006): 43–61.

Burkert, Walter. *Oedipus, Oracles, and Meaning: From Sophocles to Umberto Eco*. Toronto: University College, University of Toronto, 1991.

Burton, R. W. B. *The Chorus in Sophocles' Tragedies*. Oxford, Eng.: Clarendon Press, 1980.

Cairns, Douglas L. "Divine and Human Action in the *Oedipus Tyrannus*." In *Tragedy and Archaic Greek Thought*, ed. Douglas L. Cairns. Swansea: Classical Press of Wales, 2013, pp. 119–71.

Calame, Claude. "Vision, Blindness, and Mask: The Radicalization of the Emotions in Sophocles' *Oedipus Rex*." In *Tragedy and the Tragic: Greek Theatre and Beyond*, ed. M. S. Silk. Oxford, Eng.: Clarendon Press, 1996, pp. 17–37.

Dodds, E. R. "On Misunderstanding the *Oedipus Rex*." *Greece & Rome* 13.1 (April 1966): 37–49.

Foley, Helene Peet. "Oedipus as *Pharmakos*." In *Nomodeiktes: Greek Studies in Honor of Martin Ostwald*, ed. Ralph M. Rosen and Joseph Farrell. Ann Arbor: U of Michigan P, 1993, pp. 525–38.

Gould, John. "The Language of Oedipus." In *Sophocles: Modern Critical Views*, ed. Harold Bloom. New York and Philadelphia: Chelsea House, 1990, pp. 207–22.

Halliwell, Stephen. "Where Three Roads Meet: A Neglected Detail in the *Oedipus Tyrannus*." *Journal of Hellenic Studies* 106 (1986): 187–90.

Harris, Edward M. "Is Oedipus Guilty? Sophocles and Athenian Homicide Law." In *Law and Drama in Ancient Greece*, ed. Edward M. Harris, Delfim F. Leão, and P. J. Rhodes. London and New York: Duckworth, 2010, pp. 122–46.

Knox, Bernard M. W. "Why Is Oedipus Called *Tyrannos*?" *Classical Journal* 50.3 (December 1954): 97–102.

Kovacs, David. "The Role of Apollo in *Oedipus Tyrannus*." In *The Play of Texts and Fragments: Essays in Honour of Martin Cropp*, ed. J. R. C. Cousland and James R. Hume. *Mnemosyne* Supplement 314. Leiden, The Netherlands, and Boston: Brill, 2009, pp. 357–68.

Macintosh, Fiona, ed. *Sophocles: "Oedipus Tyrannus."* Cambridge, Eng.: Cambridge UP, 2009.

Sommerstein, Alan H. "Sophocles and the Guilt of Oedipus." *Cuadernos de filología clásica. Estudios griegos e indoeuropeos* 21 (2011): 103–17.

ABOUT THE NORTON LIBRARY

Exciting texts you can't get anywhere else

The Norton Library is the only series that offers an inexpensive, student-friendly edition of Emily Wilson's groundbreaking version of Homer's *Odyssey*, or Carole Satyamurti's thrilling, prize-winning rendition of the *Mahabharata*, or Michael Palma's virtuoso terza rima translation of Dante's *Inferno*—to name just three of its unique offerings. Distinctive translations like these that are exclusive to the Norton Library are the cornerstone of the list, but even texts originally written in English offer unique distinctions. Where else, for instance, will you find an edition of John Stuart Mill's *Utilitarianism* edited and introduced by Peter Singer? Only in the Norton Library.

The Norton touch

For more than 75 years, W. W. Norton has published texts that are edited with the needs of students in mind. Volumes in the Norton Library all offer editorial features that help students read with more understanding and pleasure—to encounter the world of the work on its own terms, but also to have a trusted travel guide navigate them through that world's unfamiliar territory.

Easy to afford, a pleasure to own

Volumes in the Norton Library are inexpensive—among the most affordable texts available—but they are designed and produced with great care to be easy on the eyes, comfortable in the hand, and a pleasure to read and re-read over a lifetime.

W. W. NORTON & COMPANY
Independent Publishers Since 1923